BUILT TO

WIN

CREATING A WORLD-CLASS
NEGOTIATING ORGANIZATION

BUILT TO
WIN

HALLAM MOVIUS
LAWRENCE SUSSKIND

HARVARD BUSINESS PRESS
Boston, Massachusetts

Library of Congress Cataloging-in-Publication Data
Movius, Hallam.
    Built to win : creating a world-class negotiating organization /
Hallam Movius, Lawrence Susskind.
        p.   cm.
Includes bibliographical references and index.
ISBN 978-1-4221-1047-8 (hard cover : alk. paper)
    1. Negotiation in business. 2. Negotiation. 3. Organizational learning.
I. Susskind, Lawrence. II. Title.
HD58.6.M68 2009
658.4′052—dc22

                                                              2008044702

CONTENTS

FOREWORD

Built to Win is one of the most important books I've had the privilege and pleasure to read in a long, long time about that portmanteau field, one close to my heart, most often referred to as *organization behavior*, or OB. It's among the few books that challenge many of the assumptions and practices about how we conduct business, specifically how organizations negotiate. This book reminds me of the first time I picked up Michael Porter's book on gaining competitive advantage or Clay Christensen's book on innovation. Books like this one, and the two I just mentioned, are not only constructively disruptive, they are also quite cleverly deceptive and subversive. Deceptive in that they take what we take for granted and force us—without being too Zen-ish about it—to be *mindful* of what we've been doing all along or not doing. Deceptive also in that everything they say seems obvious—but only after they say it. Mindfulness tends to be a bother because what you've been neglecting to see has been there all along, hidden in full sight, and because it overturns strongly held beliefs, folk wisdom, and inherited definitions of reality. A mind-set-changing book is by definition subversive.

Built to Win will upend or nullify the conventional wisdom of how many organizations view and do negotiations. Its thesis rests on three basic ideas.

First, negotiation is not simply a quality endowed in and practiced by individuals. It must be considered a systemic quality that inheres in the organizational culture. In other words, it must be considered as a *core competence of the institution*. The implications of this are huge. To take one example the authors elaborate in exquisite detail, most negotiation training focuses exclusively and extravagantly (I'm talking dollars!) on the individual's, not the organization's, competence. This single point, for which the authors take pains to demonstrate and provide persuasive examples, is the substrate of the book's genius.

This understanding leads to the second disruptive idea about negotiation, that one size fits all. Most organizations have a syllabus of stale ideas of how negotiation is done, a sort of sacred canon beyond testing or experience. The typical syllabus does not include, among other things, the idea that before effective negotiation can be achieved (i.e., getting the best deal) the organization's internal conflicts have to be managed or, at the very least, clarified. Absent that, the individual negotiator lacks the flexibility and leverage needed to bargain effectively.

The third point I'm going to emphasize and conclude with is the authors' insistence that leaders cannot innocently "outsource" negotiation to the HR group or the corporate counsel or whoever usually performs that service. Leaders have to take direct responsibility to create a deep organizational understanding that at the heart of every firm's success is the recognition that negotiation is a core competence, and the authors craft a stunningly granular description of this elusive process. The all-encompassing idea that the individual, the self, is independent of the culture is a dangerous myth that pervades most organizations. It most certainly endangers our mind-set about negotiation.

Thankfully, the authors are both graceful and persuasive in their subversive and profound understanding of the mysteries and vicissitudes of negotiation.

—Warren Bennis
  University Professor and
  Distinguished Professor of Business
  University of Southern California

ACKNOWLEDGMENTS

We are grateful to everyone at the Consensus Building Institute for creating a wonderful place for reflective practice, and to Andrew Maxfield, in particular, for quickly and creatively putting a number of our ideas into visual form.

We acknowledge the extraordinary efforts of leaders with whom we've partnered, particularly Vince Chimienti, Tom Kinnaird, and their team at WPP; and Bob Jackson and David Small at McDonald's.

Ben Webster at Hewlett-Packard has been a tireless champion and avid innovator on his company's behalf, developing new materials and tools, designing new business processes, and envisioning systems for managing negotiations more effectively. Conversations with Ben have furthered our thinking in numerous ways.

Many friends and colleagues have provided encouragement, assistance, and feedback; we are particularly indebted to Guhan Subramanian, Mike Wheeler, David Lax, Andrew Lee, Max Bazerman, David Fairman, and Patrick Field.

To Leslie, Noah, Lily, Kate, Luke, and Anya, who have patiently tolerated the absences involved in finishing this book: your love puts everything into perspective.

$$\left[\ 1\ \right]$$

INTRODUCTION

T HERE ARE FEW THINGS more important to running a successful company than being able to reach wise, stable, and advantageous agreements. Whether you are seeking to close a billion-dollar commercial sale or purchase, structure a critical long-term partnership, or foster an efficient operating environment, you and your organization are at risk if you can't consistently meet corporate interests relatively quickly while building and preserving relationships. This holds true whether you are negotiating with customers, partners, suppliers, regulators, or investors.

Some organizations have recognized this need and have identified negotiation as a core competence that their managers are expected to master. They collectively spend hundreds of millions of dollars each year on off-the-shelf negotiation training workshops.[1] Unfortunately, these organizations are for the most part wasting their money.

This book is about a better way to improve negotiation capabilities. Treating negotiation competence solely as a matter of individual skill building is a costly mistake. Yet until now, nearly every advice book on negotiation has failed to distinguish between individual negotiating skill and organizational negotiating capacity, and to explain why they are not the same thing.

In our work with all kinds of companies, we've seen how organizations that provide only training fail to achieve a return on that investment. They fall short because they fail to:

- Supply the commitment from leadership that is necessary to build better processes

- Support training with coaching and other forms of ongoing support and assistance

- Adjust operating procedures and match performance incentives to the behaviors and processes that must be fostered

- Invest in learning and communication platforms that promote reflection, assessment, and continuous improvement

The alternative we lay out offers a road map for individuals—a straightforward method of improvement for teachers who are accountable for the negotiating success of their organization. This includes division or department heads expected to meet targets set by those above them, human resource professionals responsible for enhancing learning and performance improvement, and corporate officers who must build mission-critical capabilities. The steps we prescribe are not especially laborious. They cost far less than repeated rounds of "training and more training." What this new path requires, however, is a significant shift in thinking, to a mindset that recasts negotiation as a core organizational competence, not just as one more individual skill.

In the next few pages we'll make the case that negotiation is a critical organizational capability. We'll describe the steps organizations usually take to try to improve their negotiation capabilities, and why those steps typically fail to produce results. We'll lay out the enormous strategic opportunity that organizations miss by failing to learn from the experience of their own people, both at the table and in conversations away from the table. We'll describe a three-stage model for quickly and effectively transforming negotiation into a *core business process* and for producing measurable and continuous improvement *without having to spend heavily on training workshops.*

That is the promise we're making. Along the way, we'll provide examples of successes and failures drawn from our work, as well as many years of resolving disputes and assisting with complex negotiations. Before we finish, we'll explain what different people inside each organization—leaders, learning professionals, coaches, and others—can do to build their organization's negotiating capabilities.

Now let's look more closely at how negotiations can make or break a company, and examine more closely the assertion that most organizations are wasting money when they send their people to negotiation training workshops, without recognizing that being *built to win* is a far more effective strategy.

WHAT IS NEGOTIATION, AND WHY IS IT IMPORTANT?

At first glance, not all organizations see negotiation as a key to their success. They tend to think first of revenue growth, cost management, innovation, customer engagement, and (particularly lately) leadership development. But negotiation is central to all of these efforts. Indeed, successful negotiations can make or break companies. Consider the range of *external negotiations* that companies engage in with key partners and stakeholders. In any given week, dozens—even hundreds—of negotiations are going on:

- *Sales personnel* and their managers are trying hard to secure new accounts and agreements from clients and customers. If they cannot successfully understand the needs and interests across the table, they will not be able to respond with a compelling, well-differentiated value proposition. If they don't understand accurately how the other side sees its alternative to the agreement, they risk setting prices that are too high—or worse, too low. If sales staff hit their own financial goals but fail to address the interests of their internal stakeholders—who have to deliver on the promises the sales staff has made—they will anger both their colleagues and their customers.

- *Procurement and supply chain personnel* and their managers are negotiating with suppliers who have goods and services vital to organizational success. Often, they are told to get the "best deal" for their organization, but they're measured solely on short-term cost reduction. They may have limited formal authority within their organizations but a long list of requirements and goals given to them by the various end-users of the goods or services they are charged with procuring. Once scoping and pricing are negotiated, procurement will turn the process over to the legal department to iron out terms and conditions. This will delay agreement and inject a highly positional set of demands into what had been a reasonably collaborative conversation. Meanwhile, procurement's internal stakeholders will wonder why the process is taking so long, and why they haven't gotten everything from the deal that they had asked for, even as someone from finance suggests procurement has overpaid.

- *Legal and risk management personnel* who are accountable for protecting their organization from risk and liability find themselves reviewing dozens of documents and trying to plug holes in the way they are written. No one will notice when the language they crafted averts disaster, but there will be feedback from the sales or marketing manager who finds that the deal has been held up because of battles over terms and conditions—battles that should have been part of the negotiation process up front.

- *IT personnel* are asked to develop or purchase technology tools and platforms, enhance employee productivity, and respond to a wide variety of urgent troubleshooting demands. They're constantly challenged to understand the needs of their internal customers, look toward future needs, and balance competing needs with solutions that are good enough for everyone. They can't shine if they don't quickly figure out the key interests at stake, recognize multiple options for meeting (often differing) interests well, explain why some solutions are more responsive to interests and concerns than others, and negotiate with outside vendors to customize solutions and provide effective support.

- *Customer support personnel*, meanwhile, are talking daily with customers who need help with a product or service that they've purchased. Customer support staff must satisfy callers in the most time-efficient way possible, but without simply giving in to whatever the customers' demands might be.

- *Senior leaders* are negotiating strategic alliances or joint ventures central to future market share, technology strategy, supply chain, or product development. The ability to negotiate these deals wisely, yielding both short- and long-term gains, is often central to the success of the entire enterprise.

In short, organizations that look past negotiation as a core capability do so at their own peril.

And—as the examples above suggest—sending the frontline external negotiators to training workshops and hoping that a few days of instruction will help them negotiate more effectively within their various and complex organizational contexts is not the most effective way to drive better negotiation results. Rather, the solution must help the organization to make negotiation a core business concern.

Although external negotiations offer the most vivid examples of success or failure, daily internal negotiations—or failures to negotiate—can also compromise the competitive advantage of any organization. Most organizations assign people to different roles and pay them to achieve specific results. Finance is responsible for sound investment decisions and effective cost management. Sales and marketing staff worry about customer acquisition, satisfaction, and retention. Engineers, quality control managers, and product designers are focused on the quality of their processes and products. Legal cares most about securing terms that minimize risk and maximize future rights and assets.

Given these different goals and concerns, organizations often confront internal negotiations that are more difficult and intense than the external ones. In internal negotiations, relationships are at stake, often with complicated histories; incentives tend to be structured in ways that polarize preferences about the best solution, and functional expertise and loyalties create very different, but profoundly held, opinions about what is best for the organization. Moreover, as should be clear from our examples, external negotiations often demand that parties inside the organization reach agreement with one another—before, during, and after external agreements have been worked out.

Failure to resolve internal negotiations and conflicts is risky business. Morale often suffers, people leave the organization, and distrust of leadership can balloon. Interventions that focus on skill building fail because systems and incentives are not adequately addressed.

In short, while we are process-focused in our work, we are not suggesting that organizations treat negotiation as a core competence for the sake of reducing stress. Rather, our focus is on results. *Particularly in difficult and competitive times, effective negotiation across an organization can mean the difference between success and failure.*

HOW DO ORGANIZATIONS TRY TO IMPROVE THEIR NEGOTIATION PERFORMANCE?

While most companies and many HR leaders are aware that negotiation is an area in which to develop their people, they typically do so in one of several ways.[2] First, they locate and/or approve off-site courses for individuals, who go alone and come back with a few ideas and a training notebook. Although the experience may be enjoyable, and such seminars may provide a few ideas about how to communicate more effectively, off-the-shelf training sessions are not likely to be helpful to negotiators who face challenges that stem primarily from the way their organization is structured or from the unique dynamics in their work situation.

Second, managers may wait for someone in their organization to request a course for their group or team, then look around for a provider with an existing off-the-shelf course and contract for a single workshop, usually lasting several days. Although everyone gets to have the same experience, such training seminars are likely to be ineffective (for reasons we will explore in more detail). Without any upfront assessment of the challenges faced by specific work groups, and absent any plan for postworkshop adjustments or support, the impact of most workshops is short-lived.

Third, those seeking to promote improvement may license preexisting materials (or develop their own) and provide training internally. While we have known effective internal trainers who do embed training in a thoughtful program of organizational development, these are the exception rather than the rule. And unless key line sponsors and champions are solidly behind such efforts, they are almost certain to fail. Without a more systematic approach, training is likely to focus on individual tactics at the table while ignoring the larger and knottier problems we've described.

Finally, leaders and learning professionals wait until they are faced with a critical negotiation or until they have gone off track in a key negotiation, and then hire (at great expense) a consultant to give them advice about what to do. Aside from the expense, there is no guarantee that such advice will help—often nothing is learned, and such an arrangement produces a dependency on consultants that over time can be costly, risky, and inefficient. (We're not suggesting that bringing in expert advice is *never* a good idea, but outsourcing negotiation expertise is not a sensible strategy for organizational learning and improvement.)

HOW DO ORGANIZATIONS LEARN FROM THEIR NEGOTIATIONS?

Aside from failing to intervene effectively to improve performance, leaders who rely on training and outside consultants fail to seize another critical advantage—the continuous learning that is possible when the organization adopts a common model, creates metrics for measuring improvement, and uses every important negotiation as a learning opportunity that can enhance their value proposition. In many organizations, individual negotiators with different theories about negotiation share tips about tactics they used that were essential to closing the deal; talk to their counterparts, however, and you're likely to discover that these assumptions are completely mistaken. Sometimes stories about particular negotiations that led to important agreements are passed along from individual to individual or group to group inside an organization, and occasionally they are written up as case studies that can be used as part of subsequent training workshops.

Unfortunately, we most commonly find that organizations have no systematic approach to learning from their negotiation experience. Year after year, contracts are negotiated or renegotiated with little no insight into what the other side values, which options have helped to resolve certain kinds of problems, why those options have worked, what technical and legal language was meant to convey, how well commitments ended up being met, and—over time—what kinds of agreements turn out to be better or worse for the organization. Instead, negotiators pull out a file several weeks (or days!) before a meeting and review the terms of the current contract. They might consult a few trusted colleagues about the best way to renegotiate or how to take new technical or legal requirements into account. They might make a list of aspirations and divide them into must-haves and like-to-haves. In short, they are totally unprepared to negotiate successfully because they don't prepare carefully and the organization doesn't require them to do so.

BUILT TO WIN: CREATING A WORLD-CLASS NEGOTIATING ORGANIZATION

We believe there is a much better way for organizations to improve their negotiating capabilities. It is far less costly than resorting to "training-and-more-training" year after year or high-priced consultants at the last minute. Organizations that are *built to win* invest in organizational change in ways that help them get consistently better results more quickly, while leaving good relationships in place. They provide platforms that allow for sharing and learning about best practices. They create feedback mechanisms that encourage careful evaluation of successes and failures. They pay attention to the selection of incentives (individual and functional) that might encourage the kinds of results that they are trying to achieve.

In the coming chapters we will lay out a ten-step process for moving quickly and effectively to improve negotiation performance. It requires that organizational leaders shift from thinking about negotiation as solely a matter of individual skill at the table to thinking about negotiation as an organizational competence that requires building and adjusting business processes to encourage best practice and continuous improvement. It requires that leadership provide the support, guidance, and resources needed to ensure that change efforts can succeed. It requires conducting a brief but careful audit of how negotiations are being conducted across the organization. It requires producing a set of recommendations that respond to the problems that are revealed by the audit. And it requires developing effective internal coaching, training, procedural realignment and incentives that will surmount the barriers to change.

WHOSE LINE IS IT,
ANYWAY?

The efforts outlined above require the coordinated contributions of multiple leaders inside an organization. The time commitments required are not large. Unit leaders, HR professionals, and individual negotiators all have roles to play.

A leadership sponsor with sufficient influence must believe that negotiation is a core organizational competence and commit to building a culture of problem solving and relationship building. HR leaders can help create training and coaching interventions and capabilities that are based on a sound theory of negotiation and can design learning platforms that draw out key insights and pinpoint ongoing and developing needs. Line leaders can work with HR counterparts to identify gaps or contradictions, create clearer procedures, and align incentives and metrics more closely with the kinds of results that are desired. Finally, there must be time for periodic reflection, assessment, and reinforcement of key principles and behaviors, using the experience of diverse negotiators within the organization. Often such assessment is aided by outside experts who can comment on what they see and describe best practices that they have observed elsewhere. (See figure 1-1 for the "five circles" representation of these roles.)

FIGURE 1-1

Five circles

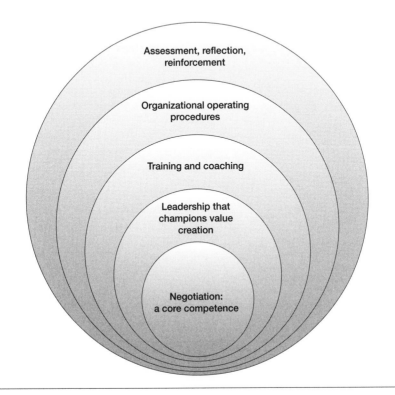

GETTING THERE FROM HERE

At the end of this book you'll find a practical section that is designed to get you started. The final chapter and additional appendices provide checklists, tools, and other suggestions about how even a small group might go about initiating the changes outlined in this book. We recognize that change is daunting in any kind of organization. But the opportunities are too great to ignore. Organizations that are built to win are those that (1) reach consistently higher value agreements and know when and why to walk away from deals, (2) achieve and implement agreements efficiently, and (3) protect relationships and reputations. Such organizations enjoy a sustainable advantage in every aspect of their operation—one that can tilt the future firmly toward their success.

$$\left[\; 2 \;\right]$$

NEGOTIATION IS AN ORGANIZATIONAL CAPABILITY

CONSIDER THE PROBLEMS presented in these real (but disguised) cases.

The 10 Percent Solution

Malik, a procurement manager for a *Fortune* 100 company, is called into a meeting with his boss, Ericka. "We've got to cut spending this year in the next two quarters by 10 percent," she announces. "I'm sorry—I know this is not going to be easy. But corporate has decided to set this as our target, and we've got to meet it."

Malik decides that his highest-dollar agreements represent the biggest opportunity for savings in the short term. He knows that these agreements involve business-critical partners who have worked closely with the company's engineering and research departments for years. And he remembers how hard it was last time around to get their lawyers to agree to language that his own company's legal team had insisted on.

Still, with a clear and measurable mandate in mind, Malik walks into the negotiation with his supplier and announces the cuts that must be made. Shocked, the supplier's people protest, reminding Malik about the key sacrifices they made in previous years. They argue that innovation will be stifled, service levels and benefits will suffer, and morale—already low on the account—will plummet. Malik is prepared for these complaints, and although he feels some sympathy, he knows that his company is the supplier's biggest customer. He has calculated that however much they dislike it, they will eventually come down to the target price.

Malik is extremely annoyed when, a week later, the supplier makes an end run to his internal customers and explains that service is going to suffer if rates are reduced. Those customers then come to Malik and complain. He goes back to his boss and says, "What am I supposed to do?" Ericka replies, "Cut costs—but don't let them cut back on quality. After all, we're one of their biggest customers." He retreats to his desk, feeling like he is being hit from all sides, and decides that he is surrounded by unreasonable people.

Are his colleagues being unreasonable? Or is Malik to blame? Perhaps both, but in our view, the real blame lies with the organization's failure to think in terms of measuring value. Malik knows that his performance review will go well only to the degree that he produces measurable decreases in spending. Other problems and risks created by these spending cuts will fall in somebody else's lap downstream, creating costs that are greater than the savings. Moreover, customer satisfaction levels and sales distribution partner feedback scores will drop. But because these are "soft" metrics in gauging procurement's success (or perhaps not even taken into account), the organization will inadvertently destroy value while it tries to generate savings.

The Last-Minute Veto

Mark, the vice president of sales in a home-furnishings company, sits looking out the window of his office. Cars crawl along an overpass in the distance and clouds reflect off the windows of the other tall buildings nearby. Mark is in a gloomy mood. Just an hour earlier his boss refused to sign an agreement between their company and a key distributor, an agreement it took Mark weeks to generate. He had shuttled back and forth between his finance VP and general counsel to make changes that the distributor insisted on. He had pushed the distributor to accept new legal language and revised payment terms that his general counsel had advocated. He had periodically e-mailed his CEO with comments about how tough the other side was, while signaling his optimism that the deal would get done. Yet, when he took the contract to the CEO for his signature, the first thing he heard was, "Who the hell do they think they are?"

Mark glances at the bookshelf by his desk, which houses more than a dozen volumes on communication and negotiation skills. "I'm an experienced negotiator," he thinks to himself. "I was skillful at the table. I invented options that helped us get most of the things our organization wants while helping the other side to get what was important to them. So, what went wrong?"

What happened is that Mark's organization failed to prepare adequately. Internal stakeholders did not meet and work as a team to identify their *collective* interests, perceived alternatives, and priorities. Consequently, Mark's mandate was unclear, he wasted valuable time shuttling back and forth internally, and he failed to set expectations and clarify alternatives with the person who mattered most—his CEO.

A Failure to Learn

Somewhere in the same city, Karen, the vice president at a leading commercial development company, is scrambling to prepare for a negotiation the next day with a potential joint venture partner. New to the job, she asks colleagues and her boss what she should propose, what the partner is likely to say, and what she should say in response to get them to "come to our number." The next day, Karen arrives at the meeting and makes a proposal that is flatly rejected. Panicked, she steps outside and calls her boss, Audrey: "They say they have a much better alternative this year. What should I do?" Her boss proposes cutting the price slightly. The negotiation fails. "It was all about price, and we couldn't meet their requirements," she subsequently tells her boss.

Karen's assessment was wrong, but she will never discover this. On the other side of town, her counterparts are preparing to negotiate, reluctantly, with their second-choice partner. "They worked for us for years, but Karen didn't seem to understand our business model or what is important to us at all," her counterpart laments. "What they proposed would have been terrible for us." Meanwhile Karen has decided that her counterparts were never really serious—but she has misread the situation.

How should we understand this failure? Is Karen to blame? After all, Karen's organization never bothered to capture what it had learned previously about this particular long-term partner's interests. Because her organization failed to capitalize on the years of experience that walked out the door when Karen's predecessor left, *her organization* set her up to fail.

THE NEGOTIATING ORGANIZATION: A STRATEGIC ADVANTAGE

In most organizations, negotiation strategy is thought to derive from business strategy (see figure 2-1).

The presumption is that training will sharpen people's skills enough to "execute the strategy" they receive. But strategies that sound like "we need to cut spending by 15 percent this year" are really not strategies; they are directives. They don't give anyone the tools they need to decide which trades are acceptable, which levels of risk are not acceptable, or a clear sense of how to conform to organizational values while achieving financial targets. Organizations that create (or have already created) the internal resources that we have described will find that they are positioned to discern negotiation challenges on the horizon, respond to emerging interests and needs, and rationally manage risk. And,

FIGURE 2-1

Strengthening negotiation

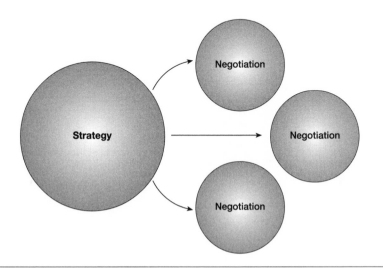

they will be able to seize on innovation that occurs at the table when a negotiator discovers a move (with respect to pricing, delivery, resource sharing, etc.) that can be propagated across the company (see figure 2-2).

Negotiation is such a potentially rich, and underexploited, source of competitive advantage and an innovation domain for precisely these reasons. Building a world-class negotiating organization benefits from the alignment of leadership and strategy with a mutual gains approach. But such an undertaking can also help to create that alignment when it is missing. The effort, therefore, can be transformative for organizations beyond the realm of negotiations, honing strategy and identifying new sources of value in relationships with customers, suppliers, and partners.

Negotiation theorists and scholars have often overlooked the challenges inherent in changing the way organizations support negotiations. Most negotiators and negotiation trainers are familiar with the concept of *second tables*, or *back tables* (the people in

FIGURE 2-2

Strengthening capacity

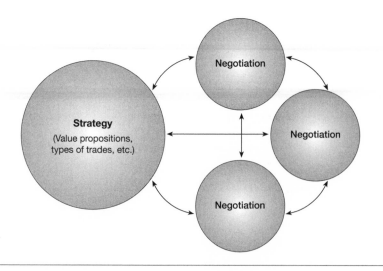

the organization to whom each negotiator is accountable). It is typically represented with a simple diagram (see figure 2-3).

Yet negotiations from an anthropologist's viewpoint are much more idiosyncratic and complex. If we know the people and communication patterns that comprise Organization B's back table, for example, we would see the much more complicated reality that confronts that negotiator (or team), in terms of structure and patterns of communication (see figure 2-4).

Figure 2-4 is meant to suggest the following common realities:

1. In most commercial relationships, parallel conversations go on within and between parties.

2. Often the boundaries between roles and responsibilities are vague or unclear, decision rules have not been agreed, and process is not clear.

FIGURE 2-3

Negotiation back tables

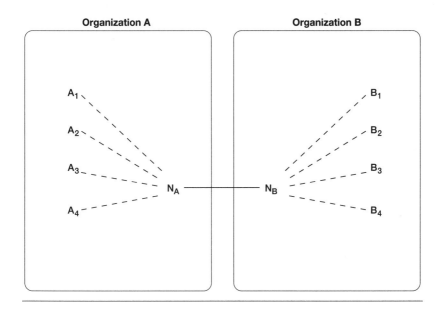

FIGURE 2-4

Complex back-table pattern

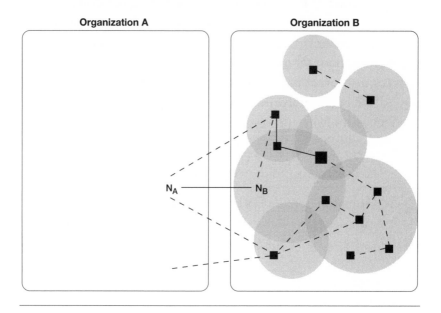

3. Stakeholders (i.e., those parties who have a stake in the terms of the agreement and its execution) are sometimes disconnected from the process.

4. There is no clear structure and procedure for gathering information about interests, priorities, constraints, assumptions, technical requirements, or benchmarks.

5. The same goes for the other side, but your side's insight about their processes and structures is likely to be far more limited.

If you are in a situation like this—which we believe characterizes most critical negotiations—then attending a training program to improve your negotiation skills (or sending your people to improve theirs) is unlikely to produce the organizational change required. Rather, propagating meaningful change across individuals and teams requires defining what success looks like and then evaluating and (often) realigning organizational systems, structures, resources, roles, and incentives to increase the chances of success. Since negotiation capability is so often assumed to be a matter of individual skill, organizations typically don't understand or support a more systemic approach and are not willing to adjust surrounding processes or structures so that individuals with new knowledge can apply that knowledge effectively.

Further, most organizations don't provide feedback or positive reinforcement for the right things, so people don't know whether or not they are doing better. Organizations don't help their negotiators resolve internal disagreements about what the negotiation objectives are, don't provide enough time to prepare, and don't ensure access to the right people or data. Finally, they often reward negotiators in ways that distort the organization's overall goals and values. In the face of such barriers, newly learned models and tactics quickly wash away.

WHAT DO SUCCESSFUL ORGANIZATIONS DO?

What is a world-class negotiating organization? How can we tell which organizations are closer or farther from this goal? A world-class negotiating organization, as we define it, is one that:

- Defines specific success criteria so that negotiation outcomes and processes can be evaluated;

- Aligns performance rewards with success criteria;

- Uses an effective preparation process prior to all major negotiations;

- Provides a common language and approach to be used by all negotiators inside the organization;

- Elicits and leverages internal experience and expertise through effective organizational learning, support, and information systems;

- Supports a culture of long-term value creation and relationship building.

In organizations that have met these criteria, negotiation roles and processes are more likely to look more like those shown in figure 2-5.

In this situation, the parties have clearly defined roles and responsibilities, have decided on representation, communication, and decision processes as part of their preparation, and have provided the negotiator with a clear mandate with respect to goals and authority at the table. The question is, how can leaders and teams move rapidly and effectively to this more sensible way of negotiating, particularly in the highest-stakes negotiations?

FIGURE 2-5

Well-organized back tables

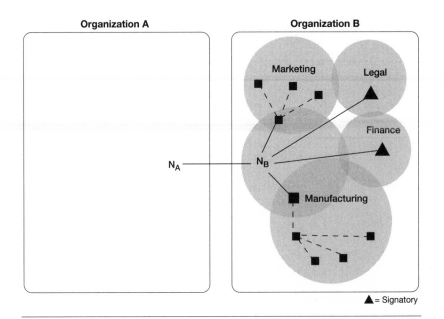

THE NINE STEPS TO BUILDING A WORLD-CLASS NEGOTIATING ORGANIZATION

Building the organizational capabilities required to produce more valuable agreements, in less time, while keeping relationships and reputation intact, is fundamentally a three-phase process. It requires *assessing* the current situation and gathering the information and resources needed to intervene effectively; *intervening* in the most effective ways to give individuals the support they need; and *sustaining* best practices by aligning measures of negotiation success with overall performance rewards (see figure 2-6).

Phase 1 involves understanding the current state of play in an organization in terms of negotiation issues, challenges, stakeholders, processes, and outcomes. It requires comparing this state to best practices and diagnosing the reasons for shortcomings and missed opportunities. It requires marshalling organizational resources to sponsor and champion meaningful interventions that follow. Phase 2 comprises steps that must be taken to change

FIGURE 2-6

The three-phase process for building a world-class negotiating organization

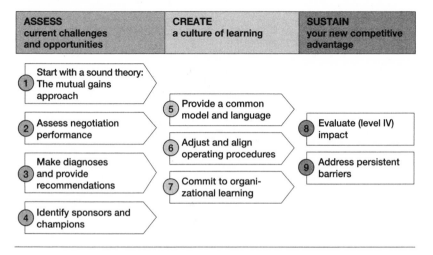

knowledge and behavior on the job. It outlines not only the kinds of training that are likely to be successful but also the additional moves that organizations can make to increase their return on investment and promote long-term continuous improvement. Phase 3 comprises the steps that must be taken to sustain learning gains for competitive advantage.

Although the model is both prescriptive and sequential, we recognize that organizations and people are complex, dynamic, and evolving. Therefore, we will provide examples of different paths that organizations can take toward improvement and talk about what we have learned from supporting and observing such efforts. In some cases our stories have been disguised at the request of the organizations involved. In others we share the experience we have had with Hewlett-Packard, WPP, McDonald's, the American Cancer Society, and other leading organizations.

In the chapters that follow we review the nine steps involved in building a world-class negotiating organization. We are sympathetic to a reader who sees nine steps and worries about the amount of work involved. Turning to the training-and-more-training model and hoping for the best is a path some will take (for those who are curious, appendix A describes why training alone is a risky strategy). But investing in an organizational solution is both more cost-effective and more impactful. It is our job now to explain how and why this assertion is justified and to describe the forms that such investments should take.

$$\begin{bmatrix} 3 \end{bmatrix}$$

ASSESS CURRENT
CHALLENGES AND
OPPORTUNITIES

THE FIRST STEP IN ENHANCING the negotiating capabilities of any organization is to assess current negotiation performance. This requires:

1. Selecting a sound and practical theory of negotiation

2. Diagnosing gaps in individual and organizational capabilities, and identifying impediments to change

3. Providing clear and specific recommendations for how to achieve and sustain better results, as measured by specified success criteria

Such recommendations must provide both a learning plan and recommendations for aligning organizational resources, structures, processes and incentives in ways that reinforce and support meaningful improvements in behaviors and outcomes.

STEP 1: START WITH A SOUND THEORY:
THE MUTUAL GAINS APPROACH

As the pioneering social psychologist Kurt Lewin put it, there is nothing so practical as a good theory. That is, interventions based on a sound theory will equip trainees with a road map they can use to make educated guesses about what to do (and what not to do) across complex and changing circumstances. The job-specific negotiation skills and processes that are taught, as well as the processes, measures, and incentives set by leaders, must reflect confidence in a more general set of theoretical propositions. A sound theory provides not just an overview, but also detailed explanations of how and why specific concepts and strategies are likely to lead to success in the particular organizational context in which the trainees are involved.

Any good theory rests on *sound theoretical insights* derived from empirical testing of key propositions. The assumptions, data, and methods used to test it must withstand rigorous criticism and analysis. It must be shown to be valid when applied across a variety of real-world contexts. Finally, it must be yoked to the kinds of outcome metrics that most organizations care about.

We subscribe to *the mutual gains approach to negotiation* (MGA), a theory based on several decades of research. This research comprises thousands of experimental studies and a great many real-world case examples. It spans many disciplines and contexts—from law and business to psychology and game theory, from economics and computer science to anthropology and neuroscience. MGA offers clear prescriptive advice based on careful research, repeated application, and refinement. It incorporates more than a dozen key ideas from the writings of Roger Fisher and William Ury, Howard Raiffa, Tom Schelling, Robert Axelrod, Jim Sebenius and David Lax, Bob Mnookin, Bob McKersie and Richard Walton, Max Bazerman, Lawrence Susskind, and Deborah Kolb.[1] Key concepts from this body of work include:

1. Effective *preparation*, which involves distinguishing aspirations from alternatives, and interests from positions

2. The concepts of *value creation* ("making the pie larger" via efficient trades across issues, contingent commitments, and leveraging/exploiting different capabilities) and *value distribution* ("dividing the pie" using mutually supportable criteria or standards)

3. The tension between value creation and value distribution (sometimes called the *negotiator's dilemma*)

4. Effective *follow-through*, which involves making agreements easy to live up to and robust in the face of predictable surprises (like changing market conditions, new technologies or opportunities, and changes in key personnel)

These concepts are our key ingredients (for a more comprehensive list of key MGA terms and concepts, see the glossary at the end of this book). But we find that organizations and individuals do best in both assessing and improving their own negotiations when they have a process model to follow. Thus, we've incorporated these concepts into four sequential steps: what you do before you sit down with the other side (*prepare*); what you do at the outset of any negotiation to "expand the pie" (*create value*); what you do before you finish and sign an agreement (*distribute value*); and what you do, at the table and afterward, to ensure that contractual obligations will be fulfilled (*follow through*) (see figure 3-1). That is the *what*. We include a set of prescriptions under each step indicating *how* to do each step well.

Although the model looks simple, it is not always a simple matter to complete each step. Something as seemingly simple as "know your interests" can be quite difficult when you are negotiating a $20 million deal for new product features with internal stakeholders who include engineering, finance, marketing, and legal decision makers, each of whom cares about different things,

FIGURE 3-1

A mutual gains approach to negotiation

Prepare	Create value	Distribute value	Follow through
Clarify your mandate and define your team	Suspend criticism	Behave in ways that build trust	Design nearly self-enforcing agreements
Estimate best alternatives to negotiated agreements (BATNA)—yours and theirs	Invent without committing	Identify standards/criteria for dividing value that all sides can support	Specify mechanisms to deal with "predictable surprises"
Know your own interests and think about their interests	Generate options that exploit differences	Keep at least two packages in play	Agree on monitoring arrangements, including metrics
Improve your BATNA (if possible)	Bundle options into multiple packages	Use neutrals to suggest possible distributions	Keep working to improve relationships
Prepare to suggest mutually beneficial options			

Source: www.cbuilding.org © 2004 by Consensus Building Institute

and some of whom have interests that clash (e.g., quality assurance for the engineer and cost containment for finance). In short, a process model is helpful precisely because it leads—or should lead—to more clearly defined roles, responsibilities, measures, and feedback. It provides a way for leaders to think *organizationally* about negotiation results and processes.

MGA is not about being nice, or emphasizing relationships over results. A theory must also be valid (or useful) when applied across many situations. Even with the most aggressive counterpart (assuming that the aggressive behavior does not present serious ethical concerns), we believe that MGA provides more powerful and effective advice than any other theory. The alternative is to default to a set of tactics that are (1) more likely to produce needless impasse, (2) less likely to generate value that can then be claimed, and (3) more likely to risk relationships, reputation, and/or successful implementation. Using the approach with a hard bargainer who refuses to clarify interests or help invent options requires more work, but (at least in our view) carries no added risk. Well-trained MGA negotiators handle hard bargainers by sticking with the key concepts listed above, even if it means they have to do most of the inventing of mutually advantageous options while working hard to respond to unproductive communication and involve additional parties in ways that create value.[2]

Imagine, for example, a team leader from a major service firm who finds himself across the table from a procurement consultant hired by his client to reduce spending without losing any service. The procurement expert opens with a blistering critique of current price and threatens that his client will walk away that day unless a 20 percent reduction is forthcoming. Clearly, this is not a mutual gains approach! What should the team leader do? Make the concession? Fight back with arguments about how good service has been? Make counterthreats? Call the bluff—if it *is* a bluff?

In such situations, we've found repeatedly, a mutual gains approach can work better than defaulting to alternatives such as giving in or fighting back. MGA offers a *third way* that is unrelated to how tough or soft someone's tactics are. (For a comparison of negotiating styles, see appendix B.) What the MGA negotiator does is to ask *why* a 20 percent reduction is warranted; *what else* is important to the client; and where price falls in *priority ranking* compared with other issues. He also shares interests, introduces issues, and asks "*What if . . .?*," proposing different options his organization might be able to accept for meeting the procurement expert's key interest(s), without committing to any. If the consultant simply ignores these efforts to change the game, the MGA negotiator assembles and floats *multiple simultaneous packages* of options for the other side (any one of which he would be happy with) in order to draw out interests and priorities (see table 3-1).

Of course, the hard bargaining counterpart is likely to say something like, "These are all terrible! Get real! Cut 20 percent and leave everything else intact or we'll walk away!" If our negotiator

TABLE 3-1

Simultaneous packages of options

Package 1	Package 2	Package 3
• 20% reduction in price	• 15% reduction in price	• 10% reduction in price
• Reduce hours 10%	• Reduce hours 15%	• Reduce support 10%
• Reduce senior staffing by 2	• Keep team intact	• Reduce junior staffing by 2
• Reduce payment cycle		• Create bonus for meeting key performance goals
• Change subcontracting rules		

has spent time estimating the other side's alternatives, though, he'll know whether to take this seriously, and will ask, "Which package do you dislike the least?" By indicating priorities that the other side holds, the response can help clarify where trade-offs are most likely to succeed. Moreover, the MGA negotiator takes pains to summarize the packages put forward in cc's to procurement's stakeholders, so that the pressure is on the other side to sort out which trades it wants to make.

It's not always fun or easy, but being well prepared and focusing on possible trades for value creation (or in this case, minimizing value destruction) is a more fruitful and less risky approach that playing a tactical game of "punch back" or "give in." By knowing when to walk away and working to create as much value as possible (even in the face of noncooperation and hard bargaining tactics), MGA negotiators typically end up with agreements that exceed their next best option away from the table. If they don't, it's because they should have walked away.

Our prescription does imagine a different meaning to the word *win* than some people may have in mind. We consciously avoid the term *win-win* because not every acceptable deal will leave parties feeling delighted with the outcome (i.e., feeling that they have won), particularly when one or more parties have lousy alternatives to agreement. We emphasize that *winning* must be defined in terms of the criteria for success that the organization puts forth. Results must be evaluated in terms of those criteria and the best alternative to a negotiated agreement (BATNA) each party faces. Moreover, as we will discuss in chapter 5, short-term wins can lead to long-term erosion of competitive advantages. Agreements that distribute value too unevenly among parties (because of power differentials) can lead to resentful parties' deciding to get back at the other parties during the life of the agreement, walk away from further dealings at the first opportunity, or act to worsen brand reputation among public and private partners and stakeholders. In worst-case scenarios, as some auto manufacturers have belatedly discovered, squeezing suppliers to gain short-term savings can result in poorer quality, reductions in research and innovation efforts, and (in some cases) bankruptcy. As you will find in more detail in chapter 5, we strongly suggest that companies that want to protect their competitive advantages must consciously work to counteract the pull of short-term financial pressures and measures.

Keep Culture in Mind

Since we work internationally, a frequent question is, "Will the mutual gains approach work in a cross-cultural text?" Our own and our colleagues' research shows that MGA can be very effective in bridging cultural differences by providing a way to:

1. Clarify mandates and authority

2. Work to understand interests

3. Create value wherever possible

4. Build relationships along with agreements

However, the requirements for implementing MGA expand, and specifically effective behaviors will differ, depending on the cultural and organizational norms. In a study commissioned by Hewlett-Packard, a team of international researchers led by one of us (Movius) interviewed experienced executives across the company who had experience negotiating with business counterparts in Japan, China, and South Korea and reviewed the literatures on negotiation in those countries as well as in the United States. We found that a mutual gains approach was consistent with the kinds of techniques that the executives—and prescriptive experts in different cultures—described as being most effective.[3]

Kevin Avruch, in *Culture and Negotiation*, does a nice job of explaining how and why this could be true.[4] MGA, stressing relationship building and *value creation*, rather than win-lose outcomes, is entirely consistent with the traditional wisdom of indigenous cultures around the world. So, to the surprise of some, we are not importing ideas from a western or industrialized context to other parts of the world. Rather, we are reconnecting people in other parts of the world with the ideas and practices with which they began. Philip Gulliver, the Canadian anthropologist, writes about African and Asian cultures that have relied on group problem solving procedures for centuries that embrace many of the same principles as the mutual gains approach.[5] Adaptations in behavior and communication are required, of course, to reflect the particulars of each culture or situation, but the four-stage MGA process appears to work equally well in most parts of the contemporary world.

A second and important sense of culture has to do with the norms and values that exist within organizations. It is important that the theory chosen is understood as being consistent with "how we do things" in the organization. The overwhelming response from our executive seminars at the Program on Negotiation at Harvard Law School is that the mutual gains approach is entirely consonant with the espoused business practices and values across global regions, across functions, and across sectors.[6] We have occasionally come across organizational cultures that (either implicitly, through their incentives and measures, or explicitly, in communications from leaders) defined success in terms of dominating the other side or maximizing short-term gains regardless of operational or reputational risks. In such cases, the organizational culture was not going to be a good fit with MGA; in those cases, we've defaulted to our BATNA.

Occasionally, too, we have also encountered organizational cultures in which cooperation is so highly stressed that introducing negotiation as a critical intra-organizational skill has been met with anxiety. "We need to learn what you can teach us," one executive assured us, "but just don't use the word *negotiation* when you talk with our leaders. They don't think people should negotiate." In such cases we can sometimes help the parties to see that effective negotiation does not require the behaviors that they have previously associated with that word. But in other cases, we pass on the assignment. In short, it is wise to select a theory that is both based on sound research *and* compatible with company culture and success criteria.

Specify Success Criteria

In part, MGA is a robust theory because it assumes that negotiators typically pursue multiple objectives, even when they claim that there is only one. In fact, three kinds of things matter to negotiators: results, efficiency, and relationships. We can parse these further to generate seven common criteria. MGA:

- Produces an outcome that is better for all parties than their respective no-agreement alternatives

- Uses a process that is efficient in terms of time and resources

- Maximizes the chances that the parties will find and exploit differences in their interests to produce joint gains

- Generates a contract that is understandable and likely to be implemented effectively

- Manages risks associated with brand and reputation

- Makes future dealings easier

- Reflects the values of the organization

These seven criteria may not always be ranked in the same order (and they may not be endorsed by every organization). In some cases, reaching agreement quickly trumps optimizing value for one or more parties. In others, reaching an outcome advantageous to one's organization may be deemed less important than keeping counterparts in other organizations happy. But having a conversation to clarify what success looks like happens much less often than it should.

Many organizations fail to make success criteria explicit, fail to rank their importance relative to each key negotiation, and fail to think about hard metrics (or even soft ones) that will be used to evaluate results. In such circumstances their negotiators are left to intuit what might be important. In the absence of explicit success criteria, performance rewards (explicit or implicitly understood) can drive behavior in directions that destroy value for the organization. For example, achieving short-term savings sometimes comes at the expense of enormous opportunities for value creation that are missed.

Surprisingly few organizations bother to go on record with success criteria, and/or organizational learning strategies are not yoked explicitly to a process model that is designed to help negotiators achieve them. In particular, we often find that when asked to describe their current practice, negotiators typically hold either vague or very narrow notions of success. Even experienced negotiators anchor on arbitrary reductions or targets that someone else has set; they measure how much "the other guy moved" from an initial figure or "how much they complained (!)," and focus on other similar tactical indicators. These may be psychologically reassuring moves for the individual, in part because they require little preparation and in part because win-lose thinking is often easier than imagining ways to create value or worry about future risks. But they should not be reassuring to those seeking better outcomes for the organization, particularly over the long term. Following are some of the ways organizations fail to create sound success criteria.

Focusing failures

In some cases, negotiators effectively give priority to some criteria without realizing it. When we mention the others, they are quick to say, "Oh, those are important too." But when they are asked to rank the criteria for the last important negotiation they conducted, the task is harder than they think, and when the question becomes whether others in the organization—including signatories to the deal—would rank them in the same order, it becomes harder still. When we ask them to evaluate a recent agreement in terms of the more complete list of criteria, there are sighs. When they show us the forms that they've used or the contract template that limits them, it becomes clear that their tools and measures do not align with their espoused theory. It is clear in such cases that success has either not been defined, and/or has not been implemented in a way that keeps negotiators' eyes on the right prize.

Focusing failures take many forms. Companies often settle for suboptimal agreements because they are fixated on price and overlook other features of a deal (like the timing of delivery, the timing of payment, the method of payment) that could be packaged to create mutually beneficial outcomes. Or they are so focused on meeting short-term targets that they miss longer-term partnership opportunities, such as commitments to make future purchases, promises of referrals or good publicity, or potential investments in joint marketing or future research and development that would yield valuable new products and processes for both sides. Sometimes parties fail to understand how the negotiation process has irked their counterparts; operational risks have been incurred because trust or good will have been damaged or because the other side is just waiting for the first chance to charge back what it feels it lost at the table. Moreover, as communication globalizes and democratizes, brand-related and reputational risks multiply. When people feel poorly treated, there are more and more ways of letting others quickly know their grievances.

Too often companies are unaware of the risks they have incurred. Consider the case of a CEO of a small manufacturing company, a supplier to an organization with whom we had just begun to work. "How are they to negotiate with?" we asked. "They used to be great," he said. "They trusted us, and we trusted them. We produced all kinds of process innovations for them, which saved their engineers millions and helped them to manufacture more reliable parts, and much more quickly. But a few years ago, new people came in and set targets for savings. They insisted on price reductions, with no real rationale. We explained the risks they might incur in terms of quality, and how we would not be able to innovate at the margins as we had before. They just shrugged. I don't think they believed us, and I don't think they cared. They don't realize it, but it's really a bad deal for both sides now. I've moved away from them as a customer, to other customers that treat us better. But I'm not even sure that they realize this. It's ridiculous."

Needless to say, we reported this when we went to meet with our client. Aside from the substantive issues, it was clear that the company's brand was at risk. The company did not want to be thought of in this way. Its people would need to find new ways to specify and measure negotiation performance and link learning to organizational interventions to those measures.

Unclear or vague success criteria

Consider a different example. We worked for several years for a credit card company (we'll call it CCC) that negotiates several multimillion dollar deals every year. We were hired to train a cadre of internal trainers who would then teach a basic course to CCC employees. We began by interviewing a number of managers at different levels to learn more about their negotiation experiences. We heard about a series of major negotiations involving affinity card agreements: CCC paid for access to the membership names of large groups or associations, such as the buyers of a certain expensive car. The members of that association were then offered credit cards and related services imprinted with a flashy picture of that sports car (or other affinity group image). CCC made money when the association members accepted the credit card offer.

We wanted to understand how CCC evaluated the success of its negotiation strategy, a task made especially difficult by the lengths of time required to evaluate whether end-users charged and paid for goods in a way that was profitable for the company. In some cases, CCC walked away from agreements but had no way of evaluating whether the decision had been wise. For many companies, the lack of a deal is considered a failure. But this is usually because the point of comparison that companies and leaders often (mistakenly) have in mind is the deal that they originally hoped for, or what previous negotiators (in different circumstances) were able to achieve. While setting high aspirations is wise, comparing the outcome to these benchmarks, rather than the overall value of their BATNA, is unwise. But unless an organization takes pains to estimate its BATNA *before* it sits down at the table with the other side and compares the proposed agreement to its BATNA, it won't be possible to gauge whether walking away is (or was) the most sensible strategy, rather than a sign of failure.

In CCC's case, it became clear that success could only be measured, and decisions analyzed and mined for learning (1) when there were clear alternatives to agreement that had been estimated in terms of their present value and (2) after sufficient time had gone by to track profitability (which might mean years). Only by making success criteria more explicit were we able to determine the kind of cases that CCC training might use as it sought to teach its people how to recognize the negotiation opportunities and traps that its strategy and context were likely to present.

Coping with complexity

A theory must provide specific guidance and tools for how to prepare effectively for negotiations, and what to do at critical decision points. But too often individuals are not given the kinds of tools that can help them to confront and master the complexity and ambiguity they face. For example, negotiation textbooks or training workshops often give examples of BATNAs that are easy to understand, such as the price of a car at a competing dealership. But in most commercial settings, arriving at a figure is more difficult. Often it must be estimated, because in many cases the value of no agreement is (or should be) a function of multiple analyses involving the probability and value of each alternative.

For example, a service firm may be trying to decide whether to take on a large piece of business with a rather low hourly fee structure that produces estimated pretax profits of $500,000. The estimated value of their alternative may look like what is shown in table 3-2.

In this case the value of walking away appears to exceed the value of saying yes to the client. At the current rates, the service firm should walk away.

Note that this kind of analysis is likely to rest on knowledge and assumptions that are held by more than one person in the organization. Therefore, estimating the alternative to agreement should be an organizational rather than individual task. A good theory that specifies clear success criteria and provides a general process model will also reflect the organizational nature of most commercial negotiations.

Organizations that have not made their theory of negotiation explicit and specified how success should be measured are at risk.

TABLE 3-2

Estimated value of alternatives

Outcome	Likelihood	Profit	Value
Land equivalent billable hours at better rates	25%	$1,200,000	$300,000
Land equivalent billable hours at same rates	20%	$1,000,000	$200,000
Find 50% more work from current clients, at better rates	30%	$600,000	$180,000
Land no work, lay people off, close office, risk low morale	25%	($500,000)	($125,000)
TOTAL			**$555,000**

They risk saying yes to bad deals, saying no to good ones, and missing opportunities to create value. They risk allocating time and resources unwisely across negotiations, making implicit trade-offs without understanding them, and damaging relationships. Organizations that are not aligning incentives and learning strategies with their espoused success criteria are also at risk. They risk fostering confusion, cynicism, and helplessness among their staff, who assume that the disparity between words and deeds reflects either incompetence or manipulation.

It is important that the theory adopted by an organization be aimed toward clear success measures. MGA works particularly well in organizational settings because nearly all leaders and managers are charged with achieving multiple (and sometimes competing) objectives. Once a theory has been selected, and clear success metrics defined, it is possible to assess performance.

STEP 2: ASSESS NEGOTIATION PERFORMANCE

Whether an organization has a theory in mind at the outset of its efforts to improve negotiation performance, any assessor it selects *must* have one. A theory allows the assessor to (1) evaluate whether and how current structures, procedures, and incentives promote best practices as prescribed by the theory and (2) diagnose impediments—in terms of both individual skill deficits and ineffective organizational mandates and procedures—to achieving the desired results with a reasonable degree of consistency.

Use Confidential Interviewing

Asking people directly to assess their negotiation performance is a mistake. As social psychologists have demonstrated, people who are asked to evaluate their own performance typically overestimate how well they've done (although there is variability in the degree to which this is true, further complicating things). Moreover, in many settings employees are reluctant to be completely honest about how things have gone in the past. No one wants to expose himself or his colleagues to charges of incompetence. Therefore, when we look for meaningful information to use in diagnosing performance, we start with confidential interviewing. We ask to speak with a sample of negotiators inside the organization who can give us stories about negotiations that have gone well, and those that have not. We ask questions based on the MGA model. We pay close attention not only to what the individual or team did, but also to the guidance and support they received, or did not receive, from their organizations. When authorized, we also speak with partners or others outside the organization who can provide a different perspective. Some organizations are reluctant to undertake this kind of external review, but we think the risks are small and the value of the knowledge gained can be very high. In some cases, when there are discrepancies between how the company sees itself and how partners see it, new dialogue and opportunities can open, including joint training in MGA, which we will return to later in chapter 4.

We use interviewing because most organizations don't expect each business unit to document what goes on before, during, or after whole sets of negotiations on an ongoing basis. They don't expect departmental managers to analyze how a quarter or a year's negotiation results stack up against what was anticipated. Unless there is a preparation process in place that documents who did what, what worked and what didn't, and what might have been done differently, we need to recreate what happened by talking to the people involved. By assuring them that nothing they say will be attributed to them personally, we try to minimize the extent to which they exaggerate or present their stories in self-serving ways.

Here is a list of the kinds of questions we ask in these interviews. We start by asking for stories. In the course of listening and seeking clarification about details, we typically begin to discover the answers to many of the subsequent questions, which serve as more of a mental checklist than a formal interviewing protocol.

Part I: Stories and Examples

1. Please think back to 2 or 3 successful negotiations and 2 or 3 challenging or less-successful negotiations. What made them successful or difficult? Have you changed your negotiation strategy as a result? How?

2. What experience(s) have surprised you most in negotiating with counterparts?

Part II: Evaluating Success

3. What does *success* in negotiation mean to you? How do you (or your organization) measure success? What is your mandate going into most negotiations? How do you arrive at it?

Part III: The Negotiation Process

4. How do you prepare for most negotiations? How are teams and responsibilities structured to support preparation?

5. How do you set the stage for negotiations? How do you open the conversation?

6. How do you work to understand interests/objectives/concerns?

7. How do you formulate options or proposals? Is there an attempt to create many options before deciding on one?

8. How do you explore or discuss the use of objective criteria or standards to generate a fair outcome for all parties?

9. How do you talk effectively about the relationship? How do you discuss ways to resolve future disagreements or differences? How do you address problems/difficulties that arise in the negotiation process?

10. Do you or other negotiators ever make use of "neutral" or trusted third parties to assist in reaching agreement or dealing with differences?

These kinds of questions provide a sense of the territory we want to cover. The goal is to gather enough stories and responses, from enough perspectives (at least four and sometimes as many as twenty), that we can begin to see patterns across all negotiations. We want to learn about the discrepancies between negotiators' espoused theories and their *theories-in-use* as revealed by assumptions, perceptions, and moves embedded in the stories they tell us.[7] Using our model of what constitutes an effective process, we diagnose gaps or inconsistencies with best practice, and use this to tailor subsequent interventions.

In some cases executives will tell us in retrospect that the process of simply telling stories, having to answer questions about them, and having even an hour to reflect on multiple negotiations was *itself* an intervention. In any case, we see it as a low-cost, time-efficient, and essential prerequisite to effective training and organizational development.

Let's come back to CCC, the credit card company. Its key negotiations were led by a three-person team representing finance (responsible for structuring the financial terms of the deal) and marketing (assigned to work out an elaborate marketing campaign), and a senior manager to oversee the face-to-face negotiations with the leadership of the affinity group. This team was supposed to generate a proposal that would meet or exceed the company's interests. In most of these negotiations, one of CCC's top two executives also got directly involved to provide oversight. Some of these deals worked out well, others did not. Our interviews revealed that a powerful focal point for learning and change was *team preparations for key negotiations.* Without the interviews we would have had no idea how to tailor training materials and recommend subsequent resources and tools that the organization might develop.

As we will see later in the book, actually becoming a world-class negotiating organization requires a commitment to revisiting individual and organizational efforts on a regular basis.

Analyze the Findings from Multiple Perspectives

An assessment should gather information from a range of perspectives and discuss negotiation successes and failures from the standpoint of both top executives and frontline midlevel negotiators and managers. Executives will want to know how their people can do better; midlevel staff will want to be certain that long-standing organizational impediments to greater negotiation success have been noted and that someone is going to do something about them. People from different departments who feel that other parts of the organization have been deficient or self-serving want to know that someone has understood the problem from their perspective. It is a mistake to uncover a few failures and leap to the conclusion that someone in the organization is to blame, unless and until that person's story and perspective have been heard.

Sometimes organizational roles and responsibilities have not been properly aligned, but more often the organization has explicitly tasked and rewarded different departments for worrying about different things. Marketing leaders worry about new revenue; finance leaders about costs, legal staff about exposure, and so forth. A business unit leader that blames the legal department for holding things up may simply fail to appreciate the performance goals and risks facing the person in those shoes. An assessor ought to help the organization normalize the notion of *strategic conflict*—the conflict that predictably emerges when different functions weigh objectives differently. The assessor can show the organization that internal conflict is in and of itself not harmful;

rather, the organization needs to give negotiators ways to effectively manage it. Very often, conflict emerges in the course of preparing for negotiations, or finalizing them, because there is no clear preparation process or because authority, responsibilities, and interests have not been clarified.

Highlight Opportunities

Assume that you undertake a series of in-depth confidential interviews over two weeks, which collectively reveal a number of disturbing trends. As the assessor, you can see that:

- The organization has made no explicit commitment to a codified theory of negotiation.

- Intermittent negotiation training programs offered over the past few years have never been evaluated for tangible impact, or provide no one theory for how to negotiate.

- A number of high-value negotiations appear, in retrospect, to have been poorly handled—that is, the available data suggest that prenegotiation preparation was not taken very seriously (even when the stakes were exceedingly high).

- A number of highly visible negotiations were so contentious that strategic partners complained bitterly or walked away. Some negotiations that were completed have still not been fully implemented, incurring enormous transaction costs. Several agreements have unwound and ended up in expensive lawsuits.

- There are no benchmarks for reviewing the negotiation performance of either midlevel or top-level staff, so negotiation performance isn't taken into account in annual performance reviews.

- There is no negotiation coaching capability in place.

- There are no measures or incentives for rewarding excellent negotiation performance.

- The results of many purely internal negotiations have been just as troublesome as the external business negotiations: small conflicts have often escalated into unproductive confrontations or avoidant stances when engagement and resolution are needed. Collaboration, even when mandated from the top, has been mostly ineffective.

A formal organizational assessment *begins* with this kind of gap analysis. It is important, however, that findings be presented back to the organization in a way that will not provoke denial, recriminations, or defensiveness. A report should describe the kinds of opportunities that are being missed and estimate the costs associated with missing them. It should make sure that the problems are framed as fixable and as not entirely uncommon in other organizations. It should also single out bright spots, including exemplary deals that were the product of ingenious value-creating efforts by certain individuals, solid or improved relationships with suppliers or partners that led to all-gain agreements robust enough to withstand unexpected shifts in the market, precedent-setting agreements that allowed the company to claim more than its fair share in certain kinds of deals, and a few individuals who continue to achieve superior negotiation results and in so doing provide valuable models for others.

Having described key themes, it is important to make the case for change in economic terms. There are three kinds of costs associated with poor negotiation performance:

- *Opportunity costs* associated with a failure to create as much value as possible when crafting the terms of a deal, or the failure to close what should have been an advantageous deal for both sides

- *Process management costs,* including the staff time and spending associated with needlessly prolonged negotiations

- *Costs associated with a failure to maintain good working reputations and relationships* during and after a negotiation.

Let's return to the CCC example. If negotiation failed to turn up the fact that the membership of the affinity group was about to grow dramatically, or its leadership was about to change, or its mission was on the verge of changing radically, the opportunity costs associated with each should be noted in the assessment. Perhaps CCC sent a negotiating team that was so narrowly focused on financial metrics that it failed to probe other dimensions of the situation that could have led to a much more mutually advantageous deal (higher volume for lower price, for example).

If the negotiations drag on, the costs of delay should be tallied in the assessment. At Hewlett-Packard, for instance, it was clear that resources spent and time-to-completion were relevant metrics for the global indirect purchasing group, but the company had not created a way to focus on them. Negotiation program manager Ben Webster developed a scorecard for HP that measures cost of negotiating for each key negotiation by tracking resources and the time to completion. This metric provides an opportunity for measuring success in a much more sensible way for the group.

Sometimes process delays can be attributed to onerous input or approval requirements involving too many levels of management. Process-management costs attributable to organizational deficiencies like these should be noted.

Then, there are the costs associated with poorly crafted deals, especially those that create second-order costs down the line because potential problems were not anticipated, even though they could have been. Consider the experience of a housing development company that measured its success solely in terms of profits on the sale of houses it built in planned communities. It assembled large tracts of land, sought subdivision permits, and then custom-built most of the houses in those developments. At one point, having concentrated on getting the permit for a first phase of a development, it found itself up against some of its own clients, who didn't want the company to build out the final phase of a planned community at the density originally intended. The new homeowners argued against the builder's cluster development plan and sought to block its implementation. While the legal details of this dispute are complex, the housing developer essentially failed to protect its long-term interests by negotiating the right terms with its own homebuyers. While the land development deal was deemed a success as long as each new home sale was profitable, it was a failure in the longer term because the sales agreements and the more general zoning and permit agreements with the county government were not robust enough to withstand subsequent challenges. The costs of the delays that occurred and the failure to secure the required permit for the planned cluster development (which would have allowed a lot more units to be built) cut deeply into the profitability of the whole project. What this suggests is that there are process costs associated with inadequately structured agreements.

Finally, there are costs associated with frayed relationships and damaged reputations, at both the individual and organizational level. Here is where conversations with outside partners can be particularly illuminating. Without breaching confidences, we are sometimes able to let the organization know generally that one or more of its partners would have been willing to make a valuable trade that was simply never discussed or was rejected because it was outside the scope of the previous year's agreement terms. Even without talking to partners, individuals sometimes know all too well that their own company's behavior and strategy at previous negotiations may have produced a gain in terms of short-term savings but a loss in the longer term. Such losses are certainly harder to find and estimate, but they ought to be subtracted from the benefit tally of earlier negotiations.

A European manufacturer, for example, decided over several years to use its size and leverage to squeeze one of its suppliers by repeatedly demanding 10 percent price reductions. Each time, it got the reduction but it also spurred the supplier to think much harder about how to get back at the manufacturer. The supplier worked in various ways to ensure that its product required many engineering and process modifications, ultimately becoming the sole supplier of a complex and valued product. At the next year's negotiations, the *supplier* demanded a 50 percent increase in price—and won it. The manufacturer had generated short-term savings, but incurred much larger long-term costs.

A similar example surfaced in the course of our work with a technology company (we'll call it Acme). In this case Acme's supplier had kept plants open during extreme weather, enjoyed high-quality ratings, and was generally in good standing. But at the demand of a vice president, Acme implemented a *leveraged pricing strategy* (taking advantage of being the supplier's biggest and most famous customer) to push cost reductions down the supplier's throat. Bitter complaints from the supplier were dismissed with the simple explanation: "They're still doing business with us, aren't they?" Then one quarter, Acme's sales surged, requiring the ramping up of production of a particular product. It asked the supplier for additional shifts to meet the demand. "I'd sure like to help, but I just don't have the resources," shrugged the supplier. The reality was that the supplier's good will had run out; he was in no mood to make additional sacrifices for Acme. ("I don't blame him either," commented the irked Acme engineer who told us the story.) Acme lost tens of millions in sales over the next six months because it could not meet demand for its product.

These kinds of stories provide not just a more balanced accounting of savings and costs, but also a chance for the organization to discuss its strategy and values; as we will argue in chapter 5, these are too often dissociated from negotiations in ways that unintentionally destroy value.

Happily, we sometimes find that leaders have recognized the value of relationships and converted them into bottom-line opportunities. For many years Bob Jackson (most recently a vice president and division operating officer) was a highly successful regional general manager at McDonald's, responsible for an area of the United States that comprised more than six hundred stores. His region was consistently among the best performing in the country. When we first interviewed Jackson, it was clear that he and his most successful colleagues were already following a number of practices encompassed by the mutual gains approach. Jackson repeatedly described negotiations in which he worked with owner-operator franchisees to implement marketing plans, technology upgrades, and other operational initiatives.

"Many times we have interests and goals in common. But sometimes the corporation's interests are not identical to interests of the owner-operators," he commented. "We do best when we work jointly with our franchisees to solve the problems and differences that come up, taking their worries and concerns seriously and trying to share information and invent options to address those concerns and interests while advancing our own. Having good relationships helps to create value far out into the future, because you gain trust, and the next time a hard problem comes up, you're in a much better position to deal with it productively."[8] McDonald's has had record revenues and profits for the last four years, and we've been impressed by the enthusiastic commitment to using a mutual gains approach by leaders like Bob Jackson. As we'll argue in more detail in chapter 6, MGA is most easily implemented when the values that organizations and leaders endorse are focused on creating long-term value while protecting relationships.

Avoid Assigning Blame

In most of the companies with which we have worked, there is more than enough blame to go around for poor negotiation performance. Most departments (like sales, procurement, legal, or finance) think it is not their job to offer tailored training or other learning efforts. Cross-cutting departments, like HR, haven't been asked to think of negotiation as a critical skill. Top management is often unaware that its inattention to negotiation procedures and its failure to model and support best negotiation practices fall to the bottom line almost immediately.

While responsibility for negotiation improvement has to be owned by someone specific going forward, it is best for an assessment to balance a frank view of the past with advice for the future. Poor (or no) negotiation training might be the fault of the HR department, but it might also reasonably be attributed to leadership that failed to allocate sufficient funding for proper training or the sales department that insisted that its personnel could not be pulled off the job for two days.

An assessor must guarantee that no one individual is "exposed" by the findings. People will not feel that confidentiality has been kept if the details of their particular negotiation are put forward as a failure. It is also wise to avoid assigning blame for missed opportunities or poor performance, even at the organizational level. Key themes can be drawn out and framed as critical opportunities for organizational improvement without attributing deficiencies to any one person or department.

Clients will be best served when the assessor has identified the salient and common problems and barriers that the organization has encountered, estimated their potential costs, and provided a sensible strategy for improving negotiation performance. Framing the problem in a way that takes it seriously, while not singling anyone out, helps to build trust that will be critical to achieving change going forward. Describing systemic shortcomings, rather than singling people out for blame, softens the blow of past failures and puts the focus where it should be: on the future.

STEP 3: MAKE DIAGNOSES AND PROVIDE RECOMMENDATIONS

An assessment must go beyond summarizing what interviewees have described. Using a sound theory, the assessor will be able to identify potential underlying problems (missed opportunities to create value; lack of analytically rigorous preparation; confusion about roles and authority; the persistence of predictable surprises; a failure to measure and reward the right things; and so forth). *Diagnosing* the nature of the breakdowns is a critical prerequisite to providing worthwhile recommendations.

Diagnose Gaps and Opportunities

Notwithstanding the amount of money spent annually on negotiation training, most people learn far more on the job than in generic negotiation trainings. In one *Fortune* 500 media company we polled, fewer than 20 percent of the senior executives responsible for all client negotiations had ever had training in negotiation. Even those managers with significant negotiation experience may not know how to reflect effectively on their own experience. Individuals, teams, and organizations all develop habits, both good and bad; in the rush of long business weeks with tight deadlines, there is little time to take stock of current practices and make room for new ways of thinking unless such time is explicitly required and encouraged by the organization and its leaders.

One type of gap concerns how much people know, and whether they know the right things. Drawing on a sound theory of negotiation, it is relatively simple to assess how familiar individual employees are with key concepts. It can be done very easily, for example, with an online questionnaire. Here are the ten multiple-choice questions that anyone who has taken an introductory negotiation workshop ought to be able to answer (each provides five response choices):

1. Which of the following is *not* an important source of power in negotiation . . . ?

2. When negotiations involve highly complex or technical elements, it is best to . . . ?

3. Mediation should only be used when . . . ?

4. The main reason that cross-cultural negotiation is so difficult is . . . ?

5. To expand the pie or create value in a negotiation, which of the following is the *least* important consideration . . . ?

6. When it comes time to divide the pie in a negotiation, which of the following is the *least* important consideration . . . ?

7. The best way to improve your negotiation skills is to . . . ?

8. At the outset of an important negotiation, who would you rather have with you on your team . . . ?

9. Which is the *least* important thing to worry about when you are preparing for a negotiation . . . ?

10. Which of the following is *not likely* to help increase the "implementability" of a potential negotiated agreement . . . ?[9]

But knowledge does not always translate into behavior, and even when it does, behavior change does not always have an easily measured effect on the bottom line. To gauge how well individual negotiators are prepared, and not only to determine what negotiation knowledge they have, it's necessary to look closely at their actual negotiation performance by drawing out in interviews how they prepare for, conduct, and learn from their negotiation experiences. Along the way, we also want to draw out whether and how the organization effectively supported the individual, or impeded effectiveness.

Assess Current Learning Strategies

An assessment should review the current learning strategies and resources that are being used in the organization, highlighting the range of opportunities that are missed, which in most cases are significant. Some companies, like IBM, provide *basic* negotiation training as part of an introductory program for all new hires. Others, like HP, make available to all employees a self-directed online module that outlines basic concepts. Organizations often provide *intermediate* negotiation training for "graduates" of their first-level courses as well as for midlevel managers. Such sessions are typically offered on a face-to-face basis by and for individual departments (in relatively small groups) and present a variety of negotiating situations in which the basic principles learned in the first-level course aren't sufficient. *Advanced* training is sometimes provided for senior managers, but in many cases it isn't clear what makes the training "advanced" other than the seniority of the people in the room. In other organizations the assumption is that senior people already know how to negotiate and how to assess and improve the negotiating skills of their direct reports. Unfortunately, in our experience, neither assumption is realistic.

Very few learning strategies are designed in response to a careful assessment of the negotiation challenges, capabilities, and mistakes of past and current employees. HR professionals are not typically equipped to be subject matter experts in negotiation, and when they conduct a needs assessment it involves either (1) asking open-ended questions about needs and accepting the responses at face value (e.g., "We need more training on how to deal with difficult people") or (2) asking which of the current courses looks most attractive, based on a summary description. When in doubt, HR personnel sometimes bring in a vendor to provide an advanced course.

Effective learning strategies take account of the current negotiation performance of the staff, as well as what issues they face and the success criteria used to judge performance and improvement. Unless and until training and other interventions are tailored to the job responsibilities of individual managers and the special negotiation requirements in their business unit, there's no reason to believe that learning will take hold in the form of better results.

It is unrealistic to expect generalists, without help, to be able to diagnose the wide range of underlying problems that might underlie a description like "dealing with difficult people." (Think, for example, of the procurement consultant discussed earlier in this chapter; that person would no doubt be considered "difficult.") In too many organizations, learning strategies consist of prepackaged instructional materials focused on narrowly defined job requirements—dos and don'ts—rather than on more general negotiation theory and its application to the full range of puzzles and problems negotiators are likely to face, not just in their current assignment, but over time as they move up in the organization. It's fine for sales and purchasing staff to learn the ins and outs of negotiating with particular clients or suppliers, and for human resource staff to be instructed in the right and wrong way to handle unhappy employees. But it's not enough to learn a series of rote moves. Negotiation instruction needs to explain *why* such moves are likely to work and to provide a framework that helps trainees understand *how* to improve by reflecting systematically on their own negotiating experience.

Moreover, organizations typically do very little other than training. They don't provide knowledge management and coaching platforms so that negotiators can access help when they need it. They don't incorporate incentives into annual performance reviews so that good negotiation outcomes, based on explicitly defined success criteria, are rewarded. They don't require senior managers to model on a day-to-day basis the negotiation behaviors being taught to everyone below them. And, most disappointingly, they don't track the extent to which various organizational norms, protocols, and procedures might be undermining the efforts of well-trained and well-intentioned negotiators to use what they have been taught.[10]

Provide a Vision for the Future

The prescriptive portion of an organizational assessment needs not only to identify the nature of the organizational problems to be targeted, but also to specify what steps can be taken to intervene for improvement, including coaching, online support, aligned incentives, clear benchmarks for measuring individual success, and approved process tools and templates. It is critical to frame the assessment in ways that underscore business-critical opportunities for improvement, the steps that must be taken to build the organization's capabilities, and the kinds of change and success that can be expected. We often estimate the value (in dollars) that we think an organization or team might be wasting, based on analysis of representative negotiations. We've even offered to stake our compensation entirely to the future savings we believe we can help generate. Unless the assessment can provide some sense of what is at stake in terms of improvements, it is unlikely to garner the kind of support that will be needed to implement its recommendations.

STEP 4: IDENTIFY SPONSORS
AND CHAMPIONS

Along with recommendations for how to proceed (discussed in much more detail in chapter 4), it is also critical to name and describe the roles that leadership will be expected to play in endorsing, modeling, and supporting new behaviors. Individuals will take seriously what they are taught in training sessions only if they see that the leaders to whom they report embrace the same principles and have declared their support for the proposed approach.

No change management initiative aimed at building organizational capabilities is likely to succeed for long without an explicit endorsement from top management. A commitment of this kind can take a number of forms. *Sponsors* at the top levels of the organization or department are needed to approve the investment and the time required to implement new processes, tools, and learning strategies. Perhaps even more important, *champions* are needed to lead on-the-ground operational efforts to identify specific problems and opportunities as they arise, to think through how to integrate new practices into current organizational norms and procedures, and to model what effective new practices look like. The champion is often a person in the middle of the organization who is passionate about negotiation—or the prospect of what improved negotiations can yield. In short, sponsors say "Let's do this," and champions lead the way.

Start with a Champion

In many of the companies with which we have worked, the individual who has catalyzed efforts to improve negotiation capabilities was not a person at the very top of the hierarchy. We first came to work with HP because procurement manager Webster attended one of our courses. At the time, Webster's title put him two levels below the vice president for his business unit and five levels below CEO. But Webster was passionate about the possibility for improvement and impatient with the status quo. He was effective because he took the trouble to learn a lot about negotiation, had a good strategic sense of the dynamics inside the organization, had a rich network of reliable connections throughout the company, and was personally committed to the effort.

WPP is a group of more than one hundred marketing, media, and communications companies spanning 2000 offices in 106 countries. Its companies provide communications services to clients worldwide, including more than 340 of the Fortune Global 500. Vince Chimienti from WPP's Procurement Leadership Team (PLT) was our first contact. Chimienti reported to Tom Kinnaird, the head of the team, who was responsible for WPP company procurement worldwide. Kinnaird and Chimienti came to believe in an overall solution to building negotiating capacity, rather than just a global training rollout. They were able to bring together COOs from major WPP companies, provide access to twenty of their executives for confidential interviews, and eventually team with Rick Brook and Chris Sweetland (who were responsible for managing WPP's global client contracts) to form a sponsorship group that had strategic insight and the confidence of WPP's CEO. Kinnaird in turn recruited champions from WPP's largest companies, with guidance from Brook and Sweetland, to guide and own organizational development efforts.

David Small of McDonald's Leadership Institute helped organize a group of general managers to initially guide our assessment efforts. They in turn brought in more senior sponsors, some of whom became champions after initial training, helping to drive and model the mutual gains approach across their regions in dealing with suppliers and franchisees. (Each time we work with a group, there is an identified internal sponsor who attends the meeting or training and helps to provide examples and links of MGA to operational examples that the group will easily appreciate.)

In every organization that we've worked with successfully there has been one or more champions at the heart of the effort. It is wise—even essential—to give the role to someone who is excited by it and eager to create change. The champion need not be the most powerful person in the organization—all of our successful champions have continued to do their normal jobs, but with some time allowance for the new role. While each has relied on us for advice, they have driven the key decisions, asked for new tools and templates, pushed back on incentives that were misaligned with company values or good business practice, and negotiated internally for the mandate and financial resources required.

Secure Senior Leader Sponsorship

One of the first moves that a champion has to make is to secure the sponsorship of the top leadership. Obviously, the farther down the hierarchy the champion is, the harder it is to gain the attention and support of the key player(s) influential enough to give a green light for the multiyear effort required. Champions should emphasize the benefits of what they are proposing, particularly the financial improvements that can be realized in the short-term and the prospects of enhancing long-term relationships with clients and partners as a result of the organizational development efforts being proposed. We have also found that it helps to have an outside consultant with a good reputation and track record working with global companies to assist in answering the questions that leaders are likely to raise. It is especially important to be able to point to examples of successful work with other companies who faced similar challenges.

Create Funding for Intervention

One of the first questions the potential sponsor will ask is, "What's this going to cost?" The champion must be able to answer this question in two parts. The first is to estimate the cost of the assessment. The second is to estimate the cost of the organizational development effort—but also point out that this won't be clear until the assessment has been completed.[11]

Because negotiation is a key skill across so many business groups and functions, it is often possible, and even recommended, to simultaneously train multiple groups (particularly those who must negotiate with one another or prepare together for external negotiations). For many kinds of management and leadership training workshops, having fewer attendees in the room can improve the quality of the learning experience. But, more important, it is critical to be able to compare outcomes and results across multiple groups. Because simulations involve two to six roles, we find that groups of thirty to forty-five work best. Once groups can be expanded to this number, human resource or business unit leaders can sometimes charge back the cost of training to multiple departments on a per capita basis. Thus the costs to HR and/or the business unit are reduced and everyone feels less at risk.

Some companies have launched negotiation improvement efforts in just one part of their organization (e.g., procurement or sales). While we don't necessarily recommend this, it is often the only way to begin in a large company because top management won't be willing to undertake something more far-reaching until there is evidence of success at a smaller scale. While starting at a smaller scale makes sense, it sometimes makes it harder to succeed. When one section of a company has the training it needs to do better, but staff in that section keep encountering resistance from other parts of the company where training has not yet been provided, the results are likely to be disappointing. Nevertheless, experimentation at a smaller scale is often the prelude to launching a companywide effort. When that's the case, it is important to select the right experiment.

The best starting places are departments that have (1) a highly competent and respected champion and (2) frequent and business-critical negotiations, particularly with the same suppliers or strategic partners. When these two criteria are met, it is easier to make the case that a new way of negotiating that maintains or improves relationship is worth the trouble, and that there will be a greater chance to pick and choose circumstances in which experimentation is likely to be successful. For example, with a larger number of negotiations from which to choose, it is easier to find a few staff members open to trying something new, or negotiation partners willing to experiment with a new way of doing business, or situations in which the relevant data are available and thus preparation and documentation can be facilitated effectively.

Estimated costs for initial interventions must be covered in the assessment. While it may not be possible to spell these out in detail until after the general recommendations in the assessment have been approved, it would be a mistake not to include a range of cost estimates for experiments of various kinds at different scales.

Commit to Goals

The goal of Phase 1 is to generate support for a well-planned organizational development effort. Unless and until there is a commitment to the long-term goal of building a world-class negotiating organization, it will be impossible to achieve that goal. However, this does not mean that a full-blown companywide commitment is required at the outset. As noted above, it may be necessary to build a commitment through smaller-scale experimental interventions at a departmental level or on a companywide basis, but only with a handful of carefully selected negotiations. Even with support at the very top of a major corporation, short-term results and return on investment matter. No organization should be willing to write a blank check for improving negotiation capabilities.

Defining and clarifying success criteria should make it possible to measure how training groups do compared with similar groups who do not receive training. Trainings should be followed up with an e-mail inquiry asking participants to report what specific things they have done differently and what the impact has been, particularly in terms of metrics that matter most (financials, process efficiency, and so forth). Assessors should be accountable for results in the same way that we insist that the organization make its people accountable, from top to bottom. Gathering feedback after the training, particularly from the first group that is run, can help to identify further barriers to change that the assessment did not uncover and lead to improvements in the intervention strategy.

CONCLUSION

An organizational assessment is the key to completing Phase 1 (steps 1–4 in figure 2-6) successfully. The assessor needs to have a clear and credible theory and process model for negotiation, one that the organization has a reasonable chance of committing to if a compelling case for investment can be made. Eliciting recent examples of successful and unsuccessful negotiations is crucial; the credibility of the assessment hinges on detailed illustrations of what works and what doesn't in the organization, as measured against specific success criteria that reflect both organization values and competitive performance imperatives. The information-gathering process should rely on in-depth, confidential interviews—and it is essential to provide a blueprint for moving forward in a way that does not cast aspersions on anyone's past actions. The report must make a compelling case to those in positions of leadership that an investment in building organizational capabilities will yield substantial returns. Finally, securing sponsorship and finding the right champion(s) is essential if intervention is to be launched with success, and taken seriously by others in the organization who are already very busy.

It is sobering to realize how little of this work is currently undertaken by organizations and their various trainers and consultants, even though it can cost a fraction of the investment for a single training workshop. Off-the-shelf training and coaching interventions that have not assessed the current state of the organization's negotiating abilities—in terms of both individual performance and the organization's systems and incentives—enjoy little chance of success, in our view.

It is to intervening successfully that we now turn.

[4]

CREATE A CULTURE OF
LEARNING

WITH AN ORGANIZATIONAL ASSESSMENT in hand, it is possible for champions and sponsors to promote effective interventions, ones that aim as a whole to create a culture of continuous learning and feedback inside the organization. Such efforts require carefully tailored training, but also—critically—a range of organizational capacity–building efforts. The organization and its consultants must anticipate barriers to change, both within and across groups. They must provide process models for preparing effectively and provide technical assistance to key negotiators. They must think of ways to realign incentives, create ways for knowledge to be managed and accessed by those who need it, and design metrics and feedback processes that hold people accountable by periodically evaluating results and identifying new ways to fine-tune interventions.

In this chapter we provide advice about the kinds of steps and resources that organizations ought to pursue and mobilize to create a world-class negotiating organization. These interventions should be tailored to each organization's needs (in view of the diagnoses and recommendations derived from the assessment), but must as a whole help the organization to:

- Define specific success criteria

- Align performance rewards with those criteria

- Use an effective preparation process prior to all major negotiations

- Provide a common language and process approach to negotiation

- Leverage its internal experience, knowledge, and expertise

- Support a culture of long-term value creation and relationship building

While intervening in the most effective ways requires a commitment to continuous improvement, it need not take up significant amounts of time or resources—and costs far less than running training classes over and over again. The best interventions serve to transfer capabilities from consultants and other outside experts *into the organization.* Indeed, when we assist organizations, our goal is to make sure that our services become less and less needed, as the organization captures and builds knowledge, creates effective processes, and learns to both model and teach its people the mutual gains approach without our help.

STEP 5: PROVIDE A COMMON
MODEL AND LANGUAGE

Unless everyone understands and can talk meaningfully about the core concepts in the theory the organization has adopted, it is unrealistic to expect the kind of systemic change that we are describing. The most important concepts at the heart of MGA were described in chapter 3, and can be disseminated through tailored training, online tools and resources, and coaching. Unless people understand *why* they should do something differently, *how* to do it, and *what* benefits will result, they are unlikely to invest the sustained effort involved in changing their habits.

While it might be possible to post a glossary on an electronic bulletin board and hope for the best, it is rare that even experienced negotiators will understand all these ideas the first time they encounter them. Unless a skilled instructor presents them, and answers the questions that come up when people first hear them, learning is unlikely to take hold. Unless trainees are given a chance to encounter familiar situations and see quantitatively and concretely how their own preferred approach generates demonstrably suboptimal results, they won't buy into the new approach. Finally, participants need to see new concepts being modeled by experienced negotiators in relevant contexts. This is best accomplished in training sessions through the use of videos and simulations or mock negotiations in which no one is at any risk of losing a real client.

Part of promulgating a shared model of negotiation is figuring out how to create a setting in which these concepts can be presented and explained—not just to lower-level staff, but to senior management as well. It does no good to train the bottom half of an organization in new ways of doing things if the top half isn't able to speak the same language, lead by example, and support effective practice.

Provide Training to Core Leaders

The ideal first move is to start at the top, perhaps with a briefing rather than a formal training session. In one company we worked with, a small task group of senior managers was assigned to find a way of improving the company's overall negotiating performance. The task group first organized a thoughtful preparatory presentation for their CEO, setting the stage for a half-hour videoconference between the CEO and our senior trainer. Our trainer used this occasion to present the value-creating benefits of MGA in about ten minutes; to be quickly followed by a series of questions from the CEO, with the negotiation task group listening in from remote locations around the world. Not surprisingly, the CEO wanted to know: Where had this been tried before? What evidence was there that MGA would work in his industry? What would it take to roll something out globally? How soon would he be able to see progress? What results could he expect in the near term and the long term?

With answers to these questions in hand, the CEO was willing to support the initiative. The show of support from the top created enormous momentum. The task group was energized. Training was quickly rolled out for leaders from across the organization; roughly fifty key senior leaders nominated by the task group were invited to attend the initial training session. After that, the training effort was scaled up quickly. Within a year, eight sessions had been held on four continents. At the same time, word came down from the top that negotiation improvements were expected across the board—since the staff were being given the tools they needed to make individual improvements, they were put on notice that they would be held accountable for the results they achieved. Of course, they learned during the training that they would not only have to make personal adjustments, but that success depended on their unit's performance, with headquarters providing various kinds of support.

Tailor the Training Materials

While a few organizations have internal trainers with enough experience to teach MGA, it is often easier to rely on outside contractors to offer such training, especially if the contractors are dedicated to tailoring what they teach rather than using something off the shelf. Feedback from organizations consistently suggests the value of complex and realistic simulations that mirror the context and issues they face. Particularly with senior audiences, negotiation exercises that focus on salaries or house purchases do not raise the stakes sufficiently for the participants.

For a global pharmaceutical company, we developed a new teaching simulation called Viatex (the general scenario for this particular game is presented in appendix D). The assessment interviews had given us some insight into the kinds of negotiations that were typical and difficult for the organization. Using this background, we structured a game in which the analytics and issues mirrored some of the common issues participants were confronting, with numbers, messages, and behaviors borrowed from real-life cases, but disguised so as not to mirror too closely any one case (see "The Art of Game Writing"). Nevertheless, when a game is designed well, every person in the room will find something eerily familiar and engaging about it.

Tailored simulations like these are especially valuable. Unlike typical business case studies or traditional role-plays (where it is up to the participants to interpret the constraints they are under), tailored simulations guarantee that certain negotiation opportunities and challenges arise. They also include fairly elaborate instructions, with technical data and background information regarding the details of the business situation—not unlike what executives usually have in front of them. Perhaps most important, since the context is realistic, lessons often involve discussions about what the organization needs to do in order to enhance the chances of success.

Training tends to be most successful when it begins with core concepts and simpler, more abstract exercises before moving to complex exercises and cases that are increasingly grounded in the client's issues and context. We recommend this approach because stepping out of context initially gives participants a chance to explore new ideas and behaviors without getting caught up in the details of the story at hand. As the training progresses, though, the trainees must try out these ideas in contexts that raise the negotiation challenges they are likely to face every day. In some cases, we provide immediate feedback to pairs or groups doing

The Art of Game Writing

G ame writing involves both analytical and storytelling skills. The analytic work involves constructing matrices that allow for interesting but nonobvious value-creating opportunities—or don't—while the storytelling part of the task involves creating characters with motives and relationship histories that are easy for participants to understand and "inhabit" when they participate in the exercise. Completing a game typically involves:

1. Drafting general and confidential instructions

2. Sharing a draft with designated client representatives who can tell us whether it is sufficiently realistic and compelling in terms of the issues they deal with regularly

3. Pilot testing the exercise with multiple groups to make sure that instructions are clear and consistent, multiple outcomes are possible, and the lessons are easy to draw out

4. Revising it based on the results of the pilot test

5. Producing teaching instructions so that the client company (through a licensing agreement or by co-owning the copyright) can use it without us present once they have seen it in operation

Note: The full cost of producing a tailored simulation in this way is typically $10,000–$20,000, depending on the level of complexity.

---

each negotiation. Then, trainees take a second opportunity to apply key MGA concepts and moves in still another case or simulation that highlights negotiating challenges even more closely aligned with the situations they will confront.

Training should conclude with what we call a *strategy clinic*—a chance for participants to apply what they have learned to some of their most difficult negotiations. The clinic offers an opportunity to brainstorm a preliminary list of organizational changes that might support implementation of what the participants have learned. In some cases participants solicit (from both trainers and peers) ideas for value-creating moves in upcoming negotiations.

The clinic draws the training to a close by showing participants that they have learned more than they know. The trainer restates one of the *worst nightmare* scenarios (stories of particularly unsuccessful negotiations), framing it as a situation in which one or more negotiators has to solve a specific negotiation problem. Participants, sitting at tables of four to eight, are given a brief period to generate the best advice they can for the actor(s) in the story. The name of the person who actually contributed the scenario remains confidential, even though that person is usually in the room. What surprises the participants is how quickly they can see a way to address the situation by applying what they have been experimenting with during the training. When we review each table's advice, it becomes clear that MGA offers a powerful framework that will be useful in practice.

Here are two examples of nightmare scenarios submitted during a training session we did with Webster at HP, along with the kind of advice the participants were able to generate in just a few minutes.

Scenario 1

We are negotiating intellectual property (IP) ownership rights with an existing $50 million supplier hired to deliver business-critical IT services. This company also resells our services, and even competes against us in some markets. The inability to resolve an ongoing IP ownership dispute has made it all the way to the executive committees of each company, with each CEO threatening to stop doing business with the other side. For years, annual attempts to negotiate an agreement have ended without a clear resolution, becoming increasingly contentious. Although the negotiators involved are painfully aware that the process is not working, neither is willing to back down from what they see as the other's unreasonable requests. They are also both worried about looking weak in front of their executive committees. Our CEO was quoted as saying, "If we pay for it to be developed, then we should own it. What is so difficult to understand? Given how much we are paying and the breadth of our relationship, owning the IP is a must. I don't want to fund their R&D and give them an asset that they can later use to steal IT business away from us." On the other side, the CEO is reported to have said, "Our IP is our crown jewel. Giving up our IP rights conflicts with the entire IT consulting industry's business model. It just doesn't work for us. I'd rather walk away than do business under those terms."

After ten minutes of discussion at a negotiation clinic, two clear recommendations emerged. The first derived from the MGA prescription to distinguish interests from positions. Internally, the company ought to take a critical look at its interests. What are its priorities? What exactly does it need and why? The diagnosis from the participants was that the company was being too positional. Were it to go back and carefully rank its interests, it would be able to generate additional options around *use of* the IP in ways that would meet interests on both sides. Also, the group suggested that the company should try to foster a different negotiating environment, one in which interests could be more fully explored and options for joint gains developed. They agreed to step back and "talk about how we should negotiate" as a way to propose a new process and to defuse ongoing tensions. (We also suggested that if changes in the negotiation process were not forthcoming, *joint training* in MGA for the company and supplier leadership teams might be helpful.)

Scenario 2

We decided to outsource our copy centers to a third party to lower costs and free up on-site real estate. In its RFP, the outsource company provided average monthly volumes for the preceding twenty-four months and requested a price based on that volume forecast. They also conditioned their pricing on our company agreeing to minimum volume commitments. Our company responded by saying, "We don't know what is going to happen either, but that is their risk of doing business." The supplier said, "We are simply asking you to stand by your numbers. If you can't, and we need to absorb this added risk, we will need that built into the up-front price."

After ten minutes of discussion, the executives had developed two clear pieces of advice. First, the company should suggest a contingent agreement: rather than deciding whose forecast about the future was correct, they should bet on their own forecast by accepting volume pricing but adding a premium to anything above the minimum volume they specified. Their negotiating team should also demonstrate to its finance department that the added complexity of accounting for contingent commitments is worth the effort because it would significantly lower overall spending given price reduction at higher volumes. Second, the negotiators should step back from the argument over price and explore whether it might be possible to satisfy additional interests for the supplier, perhaps by letting the supplier publicize its relationship, or finding other issues that it could address at low cost to itself but high gain for the other side.

Such experiences suggests that trainees are able and willing to apply what they learn in negotiation training sessions. They are often surprised to see how easy it is to apply what they have just heard to some of the most difficult negotiations facing their colleagues. In addition, they are able to step back from the worst-nightmare discussions and generate a list of ways in which their organization can do more to support its negotiators.

Thus far, we have tried to make four points about negotiation training and efforts to promulgate a shared model of negotiation. First, all members of the organization need a clear theoretical road map to guide their approach to negotiation. This will allow the participants to understand what they are supposed to do (and why) in preparing for upcoming negotiations; how to maximize value creation in various situations; and how to guarantee that they get the largest piece of the pie for their side while maintaining good relations. When trainers work from a theory that provides answers to these questions, trainees have an easier time figuring out how to improve.

Second, the way the training is presented is important. If it's too theoretical and built primarily around lecture-style presentations, it's not likely to produce results. Similarly, if the training is focused on the trainer's anecdotes and "war stories," it will be difficult for participants to understand how to apply what they have learned in a strategic, repeatable way and to respond to a range of possible tactics thrown at them by their counterparts. Training in negotiation ought to provide numerous opportunities for participants to experiment with the ideas and strategies they are hearing about. The teaching materials need to be credible in the eyes of the participants. That is, the problems and contexts mentioned in the simulations or mock negotiation sessions must look and feel familiar.

Third, before they leave, the participants need a chance to see that the concepts they have learned have immediate utility. The use of a strategy clinic can accomplish this. Trainers also let participants know that they will be following up by e-mail to ask these participants to (confidentially) report what they've tried as a result of the training, what the impact has been, and what barriers have emerged. We'll say more about that in chapter 5.

Fourth, it should become apparent during the training that the organization, as well as the individuals who participated, will have work to do (after the training) to ensure that what they have learned is put to good use. It is best if the trainees generate a list of suggestions at the end of the session while the ideas are fresh in their mind. Lists like this have often included the following:

- The leadership should indicate its commitment to a value-creating or mutual gains approach to negotiation.

- Managers should be allotted sufficient time to prepare properly for negotiation.

- Successful negotiations should be acknowledged and rewarded.

- It should be clear where negotiators can go for advice and assistance without jeopardizing their performance ratings.

- Senior management should make sure that all divisions and departments respond in a helpful way when asked to assist with specific negotiations.

Trainers can follow up with a memorandum to the training sponsor to alert them to this feedback and discuss other interventions to assure that the investment in training is not wasted.

Provide New Templates

A model and shared language should give rise to practical and efficient tools that can be used, and customized for use, in various contexts by diverse teams. We have generated a list of questions that a negotiation team can use to test the extent to which it has done everything possible to create value in a specific situation (see appendix C). Ideally, a negotiation team should be able to demonstrate that it has done everything possible (within the time and resource constraints it faces) to consider all appropriate sources of value, and to answer each of these questions affirmatively. A template of this kind can be used online to help members of widely distributed teams work together more effectively.

We offer no guarantee, of course, that a checklist like this will always lead to substantial value creation. Sometimes, because of the interests of the parties, the resources they have at their command, and their options away from the table, little or no value can be created. But working through a template like this dramatically increases the chances that value-creation opportunities won't be missed as well as the chances that the parties will come away with more than they would otherwise.

Similarly, we have developed a list of questions that a negotiation team can use to be sure it has anticipated the problems of implementation or follow-through associated with whatever package or agreement it produces (again, see appendix C). This list can be reviewed as part of a preparation process and revisited more carefully once the outline of an agreement has been reached. It suggests things that ought to be considered in advance of formalizing an agreement, with the goal of strengthening the agreement by both reducing conflict and specifying how it will be effectively managed.

Again, there is no guarantee that unexpected events won't lead to unexpected implementation problems. Nevertheless, a simple checklist is a good idea because it can direct attention to issues and options that will reduce risk, set expectations about ongoing communication and performance monitoring, and put procedures in place for addressing predictable surprises (such as personnel turnover, changing market conditions, and emerging technologies).

Encourage Opportunistic Experiments

It is not always possible at first to undertake comprehensive organizational development efforts. When sponsorship has not been fully achieved or budget constraints make additional investment difficult, the best way to proceed is to encourage small-scale experimentation and track the results. Instead of demanding that all staff move immediately to a new and better way of negotiating, departments and individuals might be encouraged to apply the new approach in a few relatively low-risk situations. Then, as experience accumulates, it ought to be a lot easier to make the case that a companywide commitment to negotiating in a new way makes sense. It may also point to unhelpful procedures and incentives that may not have been fully elucidated in the assessment. For organizations that are particularly risk-averse, there are two relatively easy and low-risk moves that can produce improvements.

First, we have seen individuals and teams commit to preparing for a high stakes negotiations in a *new* way. Once it is clear how much leverage flows from scrupulous preparation, some managers realize they need to invest more time and energy in getting ready for important negotiations. Aside from using new templates, one powerful tool for making preparation more compelling is to ask someone who is intimately familiar with the interests and strategies of an upcoming negotiating partner to play that counterpart's role as you rehearse your opening and possible responses to difficult moments that might unfold. This is a good way to gauge whether or not you have really clarified your interests adequately, anticipated the interests of the other side, developed options and arguments likely carry weight with your counterpart, and organized your team assignments effectively.

Second, at the cross-functional or departmental level we have seen organizations commit to adding someone to their negotiating team just to observe and give feedback to their negotiator(s). Again, this might be worth doing on a routine basis, but as an experiment it requires only a modest investment of staff time. Knowing that someone on your negotiating team is closely monitoring all the reactions of the other side (and will be available to give you immediate feedback) allows the primary negotiators to concentrate on what they are doing. Usually, people involved in negotiations are so intent on what they are going to say or do next, that they miss a lot of what is going on around them, especially nonverbal cues. Those in the observer role should develop a checklist of things to monitor. This additional team member can often provide important clues that can help to shape the content of the negotiations while they are under way.

Experimentation is most likely to occur when the organization or a sponsor explicitly encourages it. For example, one company we work with set up a small program for recognizing and rewarding examples of ingenious value creation or other beneficial applications of MGA. Everyone benefits—whatever the outcome—as the results of experimentation clarify what works and what barriers or problems still need to be addressed in order for individual efforts to succeed. During initial training of leadership, we set an expectation that experimentation should occur by promising to follow up after each workshop with an e-mail seeking each participant's feedback six to eight weeks out. In that e-mail we ask for a brief account of "at least two things you tried to do differently in either internal or external negotiations in light of what you learned during the negotiation training." We also ask trainees to describe the obstacles they encountered when they tried to apply what they had learned, and for their best estimate of the value these moves generated for the company (if any).

It is not at all unusual for several dozen such accounts from a single training session to add up to a financial benefit more than ten times the total cost of the training, and sometimes considerably more. Here is an example of how an individual from one of WPP's major operating companies tried a new approach based on applying key MGA concepts and created an enormous gain for himself and others.

A major component of advertising is finding the right music to go with the campaign. Standard industry practice has been to license a song on behalf of a client for a limited purpose and timeframe. In recent campaigns, costs had run up to $100,000 per song, with limited rights—for example, six months of television in five markets—and costs could increase significantly if the client elected to run the campaign for longer, in a different market, or via different media.

For an important upcoming campaign, the agency's creative team identified a music track they wanted. It was perfect for the campaign; everyone involved was confident that it would be a huge success. The agency negotiator took time to *think carefully about the other side's interests*. He learned that publishing rights to the music in question were owned directly by the artists (a group). A great deal of research was done to try to understand more about the group and their interests. Though disbanded, the group members were still on good terms with one another. In addition, the song had not been one of their more successful tracks. Equipped with this preliminary information, the negotiator located the phone number of the band's former leader and scheduled a phone call to *test assumptions* and further explore interests. The negotiator *thought about the artists' alternatives* and realized that it would make sense to *explore an option for mutual gain*—buying the publishing rights from the artist.

The early parts of the conversation primarily consisted of building rapport. The artist disclosed that that the whole album on which the track appeared had earned less than $10,000 in downloads. The agency negotiator then engaged in *inventing without committing*, suggesting that his client might be willing to pay $20,000 to own all of the rights to the track. The band hired a lawyer, and the conversation continued. Eventually, after *thinking carefully about his BATNA*, the agency negotiator offered $40,000 to own the track. The group agreed.

The track needed to be remixed and modernized in order to pass muster with the client and achieve the right tone for the campaign. The negotiator contacted a major music distribution company and put forward an *option for mutual gain*: 50 percent of royalties from the song would go to the distributor in exchange for its talents and services. This *contingent agreement* lowered the agency's upfront costs and made use of the distributor's unique capabilities. The distribution company did three remixes, shot a music video, created a Web site where consumers could download the track for a fee, got five hundred DJs playing the track, and developed screensavers and other products. These services were provided for a fraction of their normal charge (roughly $30,000) and the savings were passed through to the client.

All of the parties see this outcome as a huge success. The agency and distributor are both making money from the song. The band enjoyed a windfall of $40,000 and was allowed to continue playing the original version of the song on MySpace, where it multiplied its hits, reviving interest in its music. Most important, the client has been thrilled with the success of the campaign, and with the significant savings that the agency achieved along the way.

Provide Effective Coaching

Whatever diagnosis emerges from an organizational assessment, a call for improved negotiation coaching and support is almost always included in the recommendations that emerge. Regardless of the specific prescriptions for departmental or organizational improvement that are suggested, managers will need advice from experts they trust at moments when they are stuck. In cultures where negotiators are encouraged to seek help, and the help is useful, staff up and down the line value timely assistance. As departments begin to identify the experiments they want to try, they will look for negotiation coaches who can help them assess the pluses and minuses of what they have in mind.

Not everyone is equipped to coach. An effective negotiation coach should be able to:

- Help you set your own goals, rather than telling you what your goals should be

- Encourage you to try new tactics and take risks

- Offer support while leading you to confront what went wrong and why

- Ask questions that enable you to figure out what you can learn from your experience

- Honestly and humbly share his or her negotiation experiences, both positive and negative

This means that some managers will need help from someone other than the person to whom they usually report, because that person won't have these skills and tendencies (at least, not without some guidance). Also, some direct reports may feel uncomfortable asking for assistance from the same individual who usually evaluates their performance for purposes of bonuses and promotions. For this reason, many trainees prefer to get help from coaches located in other parts of the organization.

One way for organizations to improve their negotiation coaching is to assemble a coaching roster that includes both substantive experts (around pricing structures and other financial options, for example) and managers with good process and listening skills. Process experts may not have deep expertise in the issues that are in play, but can ask basic questions to guide preparation, identify information that is missing and needs to be gathered, test assumptions, help think through how the other side might see things, and so forth. It is remarkable how much benefit can accrue from simply having someone help negotiators think through their basic process and assumptions when they are deep in the weeds.

Personnel benefit most when they have a sense of the kinds of coaching they can get from different members of the team, and the coaching team is most effective when its coaches understand one another's strengths and organizational roles. Some organizations ask us to provide *negotiation coaching certification*, which first involves face-to-face instruction using video examples and real-time coaching exercises (using a professional actor as the coachee). Attendees then complete a predetermined number of engagements in their organization and write about what they did. This report is reviewed and graded (pass or fail). If the result is not acceptable—the engagements and reflection exercise have not provided the coach-in-training sufficient understanding of both

MGA and the role of a negotiation coach, then further work is assigned or the trainee leaves the program.

As with follow-up to training, coaching programs and resources flourish when there are mechanisms to experiment and demonstrate the value of the new process (in this case, coaching). One way to highlight the effectiveness of coaching is to create a monthly or a quarterly organization-wide eNewsletter that tracks ongoing efforts to improve negotiation performance through coaching. The first issue should contain a statement of top leadership's commitment to building a world-class negotiating organization and should call attention to in-house coaching capabilities. The newsletter should feature short accounts of noteworthy negotiations led by organization staff. These stories will be most effective if they cover the process from the preparatory stage through the implementation of a negotiated agreement, highlighting the key moves that were made as a result of coaching, and the impact of those moves.

Case studies are most effective when they are accompanied by short commentaries by senior managers demonstrating their interest in and ability to apply MGA concepts. At least some commentary should come from someone who was not directly involved in the story. Analysis or commentary by a negotiation theorist can also be helpful. Back issues of the eNewsletter can be archived online for reference.

STEP 6: ADJUST AND ALIGN
OPERATING PROCEDURES

Thus far, we have argued that creating a world-class negotiating organization requires careful assessment that includes diagnosis and prescription; effective training; opportunistic experimentation; and developing some coaching capability. It is equally important to scan for impediments or barriers to implementing effective negotiation procedures and tools. Specifically, good intentions and efforts can often be thwarted by barriers that are not foreseen or understood, including existing procedures and mandates that create confusion or conflict about what to do.

Pinpoint Procedures That Need to Be Changed

It is not always obvious at the outset which operating procedures need to be changed to enhance negotiation effectiveness. Investing more time in preparation is important, but is it important enough to redirect staff time away from other assignments? Negotiators ought to have a clear mandate and sufficient autonomy to be able to explore numerous options as part of value creation (even before these options are vetted by experts in other parts of the organization); but increased trust may be required internally (between legal, finance, and operations, for example) before individual negotiators will be allowed this kind of flexibility. While those who have been through negotiation training will often be in the best position to point out how existing operating procedures create barriers to better negotiation processes, they may not be the right people to implement procedural changes. And explaining to people who didn't participate in the training why specific changes are required can be tiresome.

It is not uncommon for negotiation training graduates to come across preexisting accounting, legal, or other rules that obstruct or preclude a mutual gains approach. It is all too easy at such moments for that person to decide to jettison all the new ideas and methods they have just learned, particularly when old habits are still familiar. Thus, a key ongoing role of champions is to listen carefully and scan top-to-bottom operating procedures as quickly as possible. Any new business process must either supersede existing ones, or be integrated into them.

Let's come back to Hewlett-Packard for an example. As with other corporate procurement departments, HP's global purchasing team was expected to uphold corporate policies, use standard legal templates, meet business needs, and complete its negotiations in a timely manner. Notwithstanding these expectations, the only deal-linked metric being used to hold procurement negotiators accountable was cost savings. Purchasing leadership determined that they needed to expand current metrics to reflect success in additional ways. The end result was a new definition of negotiation success that more closely aligned with what HP actually valued: financial improvement, risk management, operational excellence, and enhanced relationships. In short, the organization gained greater clarity about the operational success criteria and performance metrics that comprised the *best overall deal* for HP. (We'll describe this in more detail when we review sustaining improvements in chapter 5.)

Mandate a Better Negotiation Preparation Process

One of the most noticeable features of MGA or value-creating approach to negotiation is the emphasis it places on both individual and organizational preparation. This was noted in the HP example above. It is not possible to generate packages or trades that maximize the creation of value if you are unaware of the priorities of the people with whom you are negotiating. Nor is there any way to sort out your team's stand on the packages you might invent, unless you give stakeholders a chance to respond before you make a formal offer. It takes time to come up with creative ways of meeting the interests of the other side reasonably well (so they have an incentive to accept your proposal) while simultaneously meeting your own organization's interests very well.

More than half the time spent preparing ought to be devoted to thinking about how the situation looks to the other side. When we say this to audiences, we often hear in response, "I never have enough time to prepare as it is. Why should I waste time thinking about the other side's problems?" Or, "Shouldn't I wait to hear what they have to say first, before I work through the details of our offer?"

Effective negotiators know that the time is well spent, and that they should *not* wait to hear the other side's view before preparing possible options to propose. The preparation template provided in appendix C is our effort to quickly remind negotiators of best practices in preparing for a negotiation.

Although tools, templates, and checklists can help, a more substantial investment in preparation can yield larger gains. Let's go back to CCC, our credit card company example. Recall that we interviewed executives and tailored the training course to focus on team preparation. Yet each time we offered the training course, participants pointed out organizational obstacles that would make it hard to prepare in the way we were suggesting. It was unlikely, we were told, that managers would be allowed the time required to do the kind of analysis we described. Moreover, the separate divisions of the company were not used to working as a team. Each contributed its separate bit of analysis, but worked on its own.

We gathered this feedback from training participants and proposed a possible organizational response. We suggested to the company's CEO and COO that they create a "preparation facility." This would be a very small office located at the heart of the company's leadership. The most promising managers would rotate through this office on a three-month assignment, thereby inculcating a companywide commitment to the right kind of negotiation preparation. In anticipation of all major negotiations defined by a dollar threshold, everyone involved (from all the relevant departments participating in producing background analysis or vetting tentative proposals) would be required to contact the preparation facility. The staff of the facility—often relying on outside consultants with industry experience—would arrange for the CCC team to engage in a trial run of the upcoming negotiation. This might take a full day or even longer. Everyone involved would be required to stay in role. Once a result was achieved, all the participants would debrief the experience in an effort to draw the most relevant lessons for the actual negotiators.

We argued that rehearsals of this type would force CCC as an organization to invest appropriately and consistently in negotiation preparation. We also suggested that the preparatory work of the facility would make it easier to designate appropriate metrics for assessing the results of each of CCC's most important negotiations (and giving feedback and appropriate rewards to individual negotiators and cross-departmental teams). While there would be costs involved, especially to hire outside consultants on an as-needed basis, we argued that even a 1 percent improvement in a handful of deals each year would more than justify the investment. In the end, CCC decided not to invest in such a facility. But to this day, we are convinced that just a few experiments along the lines we suggested would have changed their minds. We are constantly amazed that with millions (and often billions) of dollars at stake, more organizations do not make a small investment in the kind of rehearsal and analysis facility we're describing.

Realign Relevant Incentives

People in organizations do what it is expected of them because they expect to be rewarded if they do the right things (things that will help the organization achieve part of its larger strategy). Sometimes rewards take the form of salary increases, new and interesting or challenging assignments, or promotion to a new role. In other cases, it is enough to be singled out for high praise or special opportunities (e.g., being recognized or chosen to represent the company at an industrywide meeting).

Yet in too many cases, organizations either fail to provide any reward for effective negotiation practice as measured against clear success criteria, or have criteria in place that are too narrow or produce unintended consequences for the organization and its key partners. For example, the managers of HP's global purchasing team noted in both assessment interviews and during the training workshops that effective preparation required access to internal stakeholders on whose behalf they were negotiating. Most described the difficulty they had gaining such access consistently, and even when such conversations occurred, there was no common understanding among stakeholders that their interests might differ or even conflict. Needless to say, speaking with "one voice" was difficult in such circumstances.

The solution came in the form of a restructured preparation process. Ben Webster, their negotiations champion, went to senior management and proposed a new process, provided new tools, and tried to clarify roles and responsibilities while integrating these new ideas into existing business processes so no disruption would occur. Webster emphasized to both HP and the procurement leaders who had to approve each deal that each would benefit from having leaders receive brief updates on the preparation for key deals, rather than waiting to review a lengthy technical/legal agreement along with a long story of how things played out. The new process required procurement leaders to work with stakeholders to complete a brief preparation form. This had to be reviewed and signed by the signatories in both procurement and the relevant business unit(s). Figures 4-1a, 4-1b, and 4-1c show excerpts from the presentation Webster made to management.

HP has since run billions of dollars worth of deals through this process, with measureable results: signatories understand how their best alternatives have been estimated, how HP's aspirations have been set, what value-creating opportunities might exist, and what issues or difficulties might be most challenging and how they might be resolved. As a result, leaders felt much more comfortable approving deals. Deals now take less time to negotiate (and cost HP less) because the negotiators are empowered to invent without having to check back with many parties at various stages in the negotiation process. Finally, better deals are often discovered because more people get involved in a meaningful way, providing each negotiator with greater support and more opportunities to brainstorm possible options for joint gain.

The keys to realigning performance incentives to ensure that they reward effective negotiation practice are:

1. Being able to specify the relevant metrics on a company-wide basis

FIGURE 4-1

A. Negotiation planning: Working assumptions

Negotiation planning is the first step in a process to systematically create more VALUE for HP while preserving long-term relationships with strategic partners.

ACTION: Create and roll out in Q1 'FY 06 a holistic negotiation planning process (i.e., business and legal terms) to be used on Tier 1 and 2 deals.

B. Negotiation planning: Opportunity overview

Key drivers	Proposed solution	Success criteria	Challenges
• HPIP OPEX cost pressures	Create a precise and streamlined preparation process	Process utilization rates	• "Go slow to go fast" can be a tough sell
• Deliver greater value; increase return on negotiations	Lower cost to negotiate	Contract cycle times	• An organizational shift
	Negotiate consistently better deals for HP	Deal level metrics	• Diverse stake-holder expectations
• Increased deal complexity	Enable a front-end approval process	Signature policy deployed	• Potential over-confidence in the "wing it" approach
	Create deal-specific data driven negotiation parameters	Market intelligence and benchmarking	• Access to quality data

C. Negotiation planning: Expected benefits and obstacles

Key benefits

- Efficiency and effectiveness
- Quality control
- Optimal deal for HP

Additional benefits

- Gain authority
- Clear definition of success
- Project management and communication tools
- Knowledge management potential
- Elements of world-class organizations today
- Increase individual skill level through adoption of a consistent approach

Key obstacles

- Making this an organization-wide effort
- Planning is hard work and takes time people don't have
- Sponsor availability for approval

Additional obstacles

- Access to quality data
- Getting the right people on the right deals
- Risk of planning becoming routine or "fill in the box"; need to maintain strategic thinking
- Gathering cross functional inputs efficiently

2. Gathering the required data regularly

3. Ensuring that the senior executives responsible for carrying out performance reviews actually do them

Success metrics must reflect both the success criteria that the organization or department has made explicit (sometimes on a weighted basis) and the demonstrated use of best practices in achieving them. Because we endorse the four-stage mutual gains approach model, we suggest focusing on the demonstrated use of best practices with respect to preparation, value creation, value distribution, and anticipating the obstacles to implementing contracts and other negotiated agreements. In addition, we encourage organizations to be alert to new "moves" or tools that staff have generated to achieve better results.

Meaningful performance reviews can be a great opportunity for managers to learn about new process innovations that can be fed back into the organization.

Should rewards target individual negotiation performance, group performance, or a mix of the two? Our preference is for the third option. Annual performance reviews should leave room for individual salary increases or bonuses. Similarly, whole business units that can show effective use of MGA should receive supplementary (group) bonuses, and/or be eligible for recognition and rewards.

Clarify Roles and Responsibilities

Organizations all too often find that the way they have structured their negotiation teams and processes is not conducive to effective preparation or value creation (in particular). For example, in early 2005, HP needed to find a way to generate more value for the company while reducing its organizational head count. Contracting often took longer than it might have because the legal department was brought in toward the end, after price and scope had been negotiated. Senior legal staff would then open a new round of negotiations concerning intellectual property, privacy, indemnification, and other terms and conditions that aimed to reduce HP's risk while maximizing its asset ownership. The internal conflict and resultant delays in finalizing agreement were cumulatively producing headaches and resentment—on all sides.

The solution was to charter a Global Contracts team that combined legal experts with procurement counterparts and required them to work more closely together throughout the negotiation process. This new integrated team of contracting specialists drives strategic contract negotiations from preparation through conclusion and, through adherence to a new formal negotiation planning process, has authority to execute against a plan and make on-the-fly revisions to contract language without further consideration or guidance from management or the legal department. The team's content expertise and preparation has helped the legal staff to move from positional language around certain terms and conditions to a discussion of business-based interests and joint problem solving.

By providing their negotiators the authority to improvise within a preapproved set of business and legal parameters, leadership encouraged its negotiators to develop solutions that better met the company's underlying interests. Such strategies had rarely been applied or were even possible under prior review and approval procedures. The end result was a lower-cost contracting model that produced better overall deals through elegant trades that better met both parties' most important interests—without producing unacceptable levels and types of risk (which was legal's main concern and mission).

At the very least, companies should make clear that time and tools have been provided for negotiators to engage in inventing without committing. It is often the legal department, which is worried about liability, and the finance department, which is eager to book deals for accounting purposes, that make it hard for negotiators to invent creative options or to utilize contingent commitments as a means of working around differing forecasts or attitudes toward risk. While "what-iffing" can and should be preceded by a clear statement that nothing said during the inventing stage of a negotiation will be construed as a commitment, in some cases it may be necessary to put such a stipulation in writing, to reassure those general counsels who are particularly vigilant.

CFOs and other finance personnel need similar reassurance. Contingent deals are an elegant way—in theory—to deal with disagreements about the future or about one side's capabilities. If I'm sure I'm right and you're wrong, I ought to be willing to sign an agreement that says *if what you say actually occurs, then I'll owe you X, but if I'm right, I'll only owe you Y.* I shouldn't be worried about adding this provision to our agreement because I'm 100 percent sure I won't owe you X. You, of course, ought to be willing to sign the agreement, because you are confident I'll have to pay you Y. If my finance department balks at the inclusion of such a contingent provision (because they are not sure how to book the value of the agreement at the time we sign it), it is my responsibility to convince them that there is no chance that the provision requiring me to pay you Y will actually come into play. If I'm only 99 percent sure my forecast is right, then the finance department should subtract 1 percent of the value of the deal from the value at which it's booked. Thus, by calculating the *expected value* of the deal (i.e., the odds of realizing the deal as spelled out in the agreement multiplied by the value of the deal), corporate or organizational controls can be realigned so that they are consistent with the contingent nature of the agreement.

Needless to say, it helps greatly if leaders and key representatives from finance are trained in MGA and understand how and why authorizing such moves might be quite advantageous, even if they present ambiguity in future forecasts and estimates.

STEP 7: COMMIT TO
ORGANIZATIONAL LEARNING

Very few organizations, when they attempt to adjust incentives and controls to support a value-creating approach to negotiation, get everything right the first time. Indeed, some degree of trial and error is essential. To make appropriate adjustments, it is necessary to keep close track of what was tried, what the results are, what was learned, and what further adjustments might be necessary. Without some explicit commitment to organizational learning—along with careful documentation of both successes and failures and a commitment to analyze the lessons learned—improvement will be limited.

There are four main components to implementing the mechanisms that support continuous learning around negotiations: supporting the champions, creating an online or virtual center of excellence; providing further training that anticipates more advanced needs and problems; and creating simple and effective mechanisms for sharing ongoing successes, failures, lessons, and organizational knowledge.

Support the Champions

Particularly for large, global organizations, the implementation of an organizational learning and support strategy will benefit from the guidance and oversight of champions. Champions serve as a sounding board for efforts to implement both world-class negotiating practices and as the learning mechanism to ensure continuous improvement. It is a good idea to provide them with ways to learn from one another, and to access help and support from outside sources as needed. This kind of community of interest can attract additional champions or other advisory staff who share the champion's enthusiasm but may bring a different functional or cultural perspective to the group. In some global organizations, secondary advisory groups can be formed at the regional or office level.

An effective champion's group does two things. First, it listens carefully around the organization for what is working and where help is needed. It is a frontline tool for surveying on a daily basis how training, coaching, and other efforts are being used and received. Second, it provides a way for champions and outside consultants to test ideas and describe the steps that might come next. An active and cross-functional group can anticipate political and alignment issues that might derail negotiation improvement efforts, and help the champions craft proposals in ways that increase the odds of success. Advisory groups can meet via teleconference or conference calls, and depending on the size of the organization and the speed of the change efforts, convene anywhere from monthly to twice a year.

Document Successes (and Failures)

There will be resistance to efforts to document the success and failure of experiments. Those whose difficulties might be instructive to others will not want their shortcomings broadcast widely, which is a loss for the organization; usually, more can be learned from failures than from successes. To increase comfort with sharing failures, names of individuals can be masked. Stories can be disguised or altered in ways that preserve the statement of the problem, the moves made, and the lessons learned. Someone from the champion's team, or an appropriate consultant, can provide a short analysis of each case—even if the stories are told by those involved—to ensure that the appropriate lessons are clear. Such commentary should be constructive and sympathetic in tone, so that no one feels blamed. (Note that when confidentiality has been preserved during the assessment phase, employees will be more likely to come forward to discuss the results of experimentation.)

There is sometimes also resistance to publishing success stories. The individuals involved may worry that expectations will be set too high with regard to their future performance, or that the success will somehow filter back to their client or supplier counterpart. They may also be concerned that others will be jealous of their success and seek to sabotage them in the future. Thus it may also make sense to present success stories anonymously.

Create a Virtual Center of Excellence

The eNewsletter format described above can be an effective and inexpensive mechanism for maintaining communication about negotiation topics, successes, failures, and needs. Each issue can contain one or more articles on topics of interest; brief cases put forward by different people in the organization (or by experts from outside the organization); and short commentaries by negotiation experts or leaders. The eNewsletter can also remind readers where to find downloadable tools and templates, whom they can turn to for coaching, and what learning opportunities may be coming up. As another option, it can be accompanied online by a blog written by someone in-house or outside the organization to encourage the posting of questions and requests for assistance.

An eNewsletter is a relatively simple and inexpensive mechanism for promoting organizational learning. However, we think that a slightly more significant investment can produce an enormously powerful resource for the organization. New technologies are now making possible new *virtual* opportunities for collaboration, learning, and support or coaching from experts (from outside and inside the organization). We are now experimenting with technologies that create secure interactive tools for communication and learning; and secure pages or "rooms" where particular groups or subsidiaries can work through interactive tools to leverage distributed knowledge; and enable rich media-content learning experiences. Some of these technologies allow designated administrators from the organization to mine conversations and inquiries for patterns and trends and to monitor performance. Such technologies also permit more effective sharing of knowledge about counterparts, their interests, helpful benchmarks, past technical and legal precedents and requirements, and so forth.

A *virtual center of excellence* (COE) has two main functional platforms. First, it is an online learning portal where all tools, templates, video lectures, podcasts, FAQs, articles, blogs, and discussion transcripts can be captured, organized, and archived.

This allows everyone from first-time hires to the most experienced negotiators to guide themselves toward the resources they need. Content can also be rated by users for quality and helpfulness; this allows for continuous improvement to the materials. Having such content allows users to:

1. Review ideas covered in the initial training

2. Access various templates introduced in the training (along with instructions for their use)

3. View illustrations or "worked examples" of ways to handle typical problems or difficulties

4. Name problems and request additional help or examples that may be missing or underrepresented

Figures 4-2 and 4-3 are screen captures from this kind of tool. Figure 4-2 shows a page from an online learning center; figure 4-3 shows a drag-and-drop assessment tool (a "q-sort" exercise we've developed to measure tendencies to use various MGA behaviors).

The second kind of platform, which leverages social networking technologies, allows people to work together more effectively, particularly across regions and countries. In a secured user space, multiple parties (sometimes globally distributed) can work together to run through a preparation tool, brainstorm new value-creating moves, and learn what is collectively known about the other side and its needs. Such online collaboration can generate a summary document that everyone can take to a negotiation. Figure 4-4 presents an example of a workflow tool that allows users from many locations to plan together for an upcoming negotiation.

Moreover, this second type of platform allows both individuals and teams to pose questions to a designated community of users, and to get answers quickly, from inside and outside the organization, from coaches and other experts. Embedded search engines can track inquiries in terms of pre-assigned keywords, and show quickly which topics are more active and which answers have

FIGURE 4-2

Learning Portal home page

| Dashboard | **Learning** | Community | Workspace | search |

MGA Learning Portal

Did you know...you have not registered your personal learning plan

The Mutual Gains Approach to Negotiation

Increase your negotiation skills by studying the four phases of the Mutual Gains Approach. Each phase and subtopic includes videos, case studies, resources, and quizzes to help you build your knowledge and abilities. Roll over each phase for a list of subtopics. Click to view the learning modules.

Prepare | Create Value | Distribute Value | Follow Through

Resource Library

>> Videos

Select a Video

→ Tips for Preparation

→ Interview with Hal Movius

→ Collaborating despite Competition

(view all videos)

>> Self Assessment

Learn from yourself.
Applying the Mutual Gains Approach to Negotiation will require you to look closely at your skills and behaviors. Using this self-assessment tool, you can identify your areas of strength and weakness and make a personal learning plan.   (take test)

>> Links and Resources

CompanyWeb	Contracts	Trends	CBI
xyzprocurement.net	Templates	IMS Magazine	cbuilding.org
Handbook	Legal	Yearly Reports	Upcoming events
Policies		CEO's Blog	Coach's blog

RSS Feeds

>> Articles

Advertising Contracts `new`
In response to the Spring 2008 survey regarding most significant negotiation challenges, I would like to discuss methods to "set the table" in your next advertising negotiation...

Four Value Creating Moves at the Table `new`
Larry Susskind discusses four essential moves you can make in your next negotiation. What's your reaction to the assertion that it's possible to uncover hidden value that improves each side...

Sean Holland Discusses Lessons Learned
After two years of carefully implementing the Mutual Gains Approach and charting key negotiation processes, Sean Holland, VP of North America Sales, introduces two key lessons...   (view articles)

>> FAQs

How do I calculate my BATNA?

What if there's no value to create?

Who should be involved in preparation?

(view more)

Podcasts

2008 Negotiations in Review
John Workman highlights four successful negotiations and demonstrates...
Watch | Subscribe   (view more)

Source: © 2008 Consensus Building Institute. Some rights reserved.

FIGURE 4-3

Interactive assessment tool

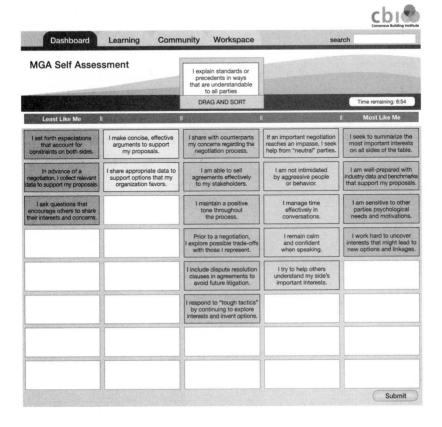

proven most useful. This allows an additional set of materials and conversations to accrue, and gives organizations a powerful new way to identify future needs and to quickly address them.

While virtual coaching and advice cannot always replace the richness of face-to-face communication, they can present multiple points of view quickly from across the organization. A COE need not be built or staffed by full-time company personnel. Outside advisers can develop and mount it. Trained managers with the best grasp of negotiation theory and practice can be assigned to

FIGURE 4-4

Workflow tool

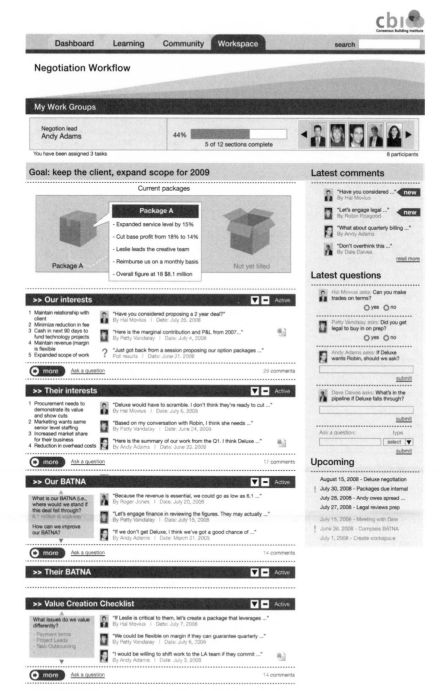

Source: © 2008 Consensus Building Institute. Some rights reserved.

devote a few hours a week to responding to requests for assistance, backed up by whatever outside negotiation consultants may be required.

Hewlett-Packard has developed what it calls the *Negotiator's Garage* as an online resource for any and all negotiators in the company. The Garage is a dynamic virtual environment that provides experienced negotiators real-time access to the resources they need to be successful. This includes on-demand training resources, tools, and templates for strategy preparation and execution, a manager's corner with a focus on driving negotiation performance through effective coaching, and a repository for sharing and storing negotiation histories. The Garage also provides HP leaders with a unified vision and working definition of what it will take for their company to be a world-class negotiating organization.

Roll Out Additional Training as Needed

From questions gathered through an advisory group, an eNewsletter, and/or a COE, it should be possible to identify additional puzzles or issues to address in follow-up training. This does not necessarily mean that follow-up training is required for everyone in the organization. Some examples of more advanced training might include:

- Value-creation strategies in highly constrained negotiations

- Techniques for creating nearly self-enforcing agreements (deals that both sides are eager to implement because their interests have been met; and that have incorporated incentives and controls that make noncompliance costly)

- Joint fact-finding techniques for highly technical negotiations

Such courses can be developed by outside specialists in conjunction with HR champions and the advisory team. Or internal trainers can deliver them, perhaps with occasional help from outside consultants or trainers. At WPP, Tom Kinnaird and his team created a one-day course based on the two-day MGA course we delivered for many of WPP's leaders. Kinnaird's team delivers the course on demand (for free—WPP pays for Kinnaird's time but its operating companies can bring him in-house). Over the last two years Kinnaird and his team have delivered more than 150 workshops to more than 2000 people around the world, for only the cost of their time and a small investment in some teaching simulations. This is an extremely efficient way of reaching thousands of WPP's employees worldwide. Moreover, because Kinnaird has a view across the companies, he is able to bring highly relevant examples from their world to bear.

Some of WPP's companies have gone even farther. Ogilvy & Mather, for example, has formed regional learning groups and rolled out training in Europe and Asia, using elements of our MGA course but with tailoring for Ogilvy audiences. We applaud their efforts and have occasionally provided guidance toward resources or in answering difficult questions. But for the most part, they have taken ownership of the initiative and run with it.

Our relationship with the American Cancer Society (ACS) began as a month-long project to provide tailored training for executive managing directors from regional offices all over the country. ACS is one of the country's largest and most influential nonprofit organizations, with over two million volunteers. The initial one-day course catalyzed an organization-wide commitment to build the negotiation skills of all ACS staff and volunteers. Two separate courses were designed. The first was a one-day basic negotiation skills course for volunteers and staff. We trained a team of ACS staff at regional and field offices to deliver this course, which they then rolled out regionally. Some of the workshops were held during divisional and national conference events, while others were conducted as stand-alones. The second course was a two-day advanced workshop for staff and volunteers who had taken the basic course and were facing especially difficult negotiation challenges. This was given once a year by experienced external trainers. The response to the overall effort was very positive and quite cost-effective for ACS. It would not have been possible to plan the second-level course until after a large portion of the organization had a chance to complete the first-level course, experiment with what they learned, provide new resources, and formulate a request for additional assistance.

One particularly powerful form of training is extremely underutilized—*joint training in negotiation with a commercial counterpart, such as a major (repeat) customer.* We have used joint training in contract bargaining, after a strike and before the next scheduled round of negotiations, to bring union and management teams together. A two- or three-day encounter has completely altered the teams' subsequent approach to contract negotiations. Time is no longer wasted on long diatribes accusing the other side of past misdeeds. Proposals aimed at maximizing joint gains (by changing the way negotiations are structured) can be developed jointly. While there is still tension during subsequent negotiations, when it comes time to distribute the value they have created, both sides will be a lot more confident that they will be able to avoid suboptimal agreements. This is the kind of thing that can be tried as a one-time experiment. If it works, both sides can talk about incorporating the results into new ground rules governing their ongoing interaction.

Joint training can be a somewhat frightening suggestion to managers who view negotiations solely in win-lose terms. They fear that joint training with their "adversaries" in advance of an annual contract renewal, for example, will reveal secrets or weaknesses that can be used against them. What they don't realize is that when both sides are aware of (and in best cases, committed to using) a mutual gains approach to negotiation, it is much easier to engage in value-creating moves, and much more likely that relationships will be preserved even when difficult value-distribution questions come into play. A one-day joint training for negotiating teams from both sides need not focus on the actual details of an upcoming transaction. Rather, it sometimes works best when participants work through entirely unrelated simulations and cases (that nonetheless address the same kinds of problems and solutions they usually encounter). Stepping away from the context they are used to can free them to imagine negotiations in a new way. Then, as the day progresses, they can talk about how they want to apply these ideas in their own situation.

Our notion of *joint training* should be distinguished from other kinds of events that might, on the surface, be misconstrued as something similar. We are well aware of supplier management programs, for example, and other related programs to which partners are invited. Most seem to offer a lot of happy talk about partnership, and sometimes team-building exercises and other activities designed to enhance relationships. We don't object to relationship building, but we frankly feel this is a poor use of resources and senior management's time. (We heard about one organization that spent $3 million on such programs, which one employee called "schmoozathons.") What partners need is a way to work together to manage the conflict that is going to come up at every stage of their relationship. They need a theory of how best to deal with their differences with practical tools and templates. We don't think most "events" will provide such learning or actually change behaviors that are causing difficulty.

At the time of this writing, McDonald's is piloting joint training in negotiation for its regional staff and their business partners, the individual owner-operators (franchisees) of its stores. We'll be eager to see the effects of this initiative.

CONCLUSIONS

Intervening to improve organizational negotiation capabilities require sustained commitments—lasting years, rather than months. Intervention need not cost a fortune; in fact, everything we have described costs about what five negotiation training workshops might cost, when trainee travel costs and time away from the job are included. The results, however, should begin to show up on the bottom line almost immediately.

Here is an example of how to create a disguised but meaningful case for use in eNewsletters, or within a virtual center of excellence. The case was provided by a leader we had trained a few months earlier. The business leader was interviewed by the initiative Champions, who then drafted the case. We then disguised the details, so that the case could be shared, and highlighted the moves and thinking that seemed to exemplify successful experimentation with MGA. The disguised draft was then verified by the interviewee as having preserved the key facts and outcomes from the original write-up.

The Annual KeplerHausen Fee Negotiation

Sean was doing his best to remain optimistic. After all, he had tried some new things in his negotiation that morning with a start-up outdoor equipment boutique, and the results had been better than he might have hoped. But a month ahead, real trouble was looming, and as he sat looking out the window on his flight home, Sean's optimism began to give way to anxiety. As commercial manager at Bancroft & Scully, a global advertising firm, he would again lead the annual fee negotiation with one of Bancroft's largest clients, the consumer electronics giant KeplerHausen.

Like a handful of other executives at Bancroft & Scully, Sean had recently attended a negotiation workshop that introduced the mutual gains approach, a process that stresses preparation and value creation. The process model described in the workshop had seemed to Sean to be grounded in good common sense; yet it was unnerving to realize how profoundly actual practice deviated from the ideals—especially in the relationship with KeplerHausen.

Last year's fee negotiation had ended badly. Sean had certainly achieved good results for Bancroft & Scully, but only after twelve hours of aggressive negotiation, characterized by highly positional behavior from both Bancroft's team and the

Kepler procurement representative. The negotiation had ended in a showdown, with Sean deliberately—albeit reluctantly—provoking an impasse by refusing to agree to Kepler's radical proposal. Ultimately Kepler had backed down, but not before personal relationships had soured. It stung Sean personally when, following the negotiation, a Kepler VP wrote to Craig Cooper (regional vice president for EMR, Bancroft's parent company, and owner of the overall Kepler commercial relationship) to condemn Bancroft's hardnosed approach. But Sean himself recognized the problem, remarking to a colleague, "We were both playing the wrong game; the negotiation process really wasn't in the best interest of either side." With a soured relationship and a turbulent financial year for Kepler, this year's fee negotiation threatened to be even worse.

Sean contemplated Bancroft's history with Kepler. During the past twenty years, and particularly during a decade of continuous growth in world markets early on, Kepler had made agreements with EMR agencies for a host of services, eventually drawing up an exclusive global contract. The contract had been renegotiated six years ago, changing the commercial basis of the account from commissions to fees and providing for an annual renegotiation of the terms on which the fees were calculated, according to a series of regional addenda. However, Sean recognized that the upcoming negotiations would take place at the end of the two worst years his client had ever seen—insiders estimated that Kepler would face millions of euros in operating losses and over thousands of layoffs. Not surprisingly, Kepler had been signaling the need for its suppliers to share the burden.

Moreover, Kepler indicated it would be bringing five senior executives to the negotiation, including the global head of procurement. Predicting their behavior was especially difficult, since three of the five were new to their positions and one newcomer was rumored to be hotheaded and domineering. But this much was sure: Kepler wouldn't permit an impasse and Sean would be scrutinized from both sides.

Thinking back on what he had learned about the mutual gains approach, but without his training materials at hand, Sean recalled a few concepts and alternately daydreamed and scribbled as he tried to visualize their application to the upcoming Kepler negotiation.

Sean first considered his BATNA—best alternative to a negotiated agreement—and then Kepler's. Neither was good. Bancroft could not afford to lose the Kepler account, for both financial and political reasons. On the other hand, Kepler had little freedom to take its business elsewhere, particularly since Bancroft had been delivering excellent work. While examining BATNAs did balance his perception of power, it was exploring the ZOPA—the zone of possible agreement—that started to open a fresh perspective in Sean's mind.

Opening his laptop, Sean typed in ranges of possible outcomes for each of the major variables that would affect Bancroft's total fee, gradually uncovering an overall ZOPA. Still, the picture looked lopsided. His experience from the previous year told him the discussion would gravitate to numbers immediately unless he framed the dialogue in terms of value creation. So he began to list ways in which Bancroft had added value or generated efficiency improvements during the past year, all of which could be quantified and rolled up into a bookable savings for the Kepler procurement client, and give Sean grounds to defend Bancroft's overhead rate.

As the plane landed, Sean realized he had made a good start but could use help. The following Monday, he called on Tim Wainwright, head of commercial services for EMR, for coaching. Tim helped Sean create a presentation highlighting how Bancroft had added value or improved efficiency in each of five fee categories. He also helped Sean experiment with different role-playing scenarios and explored how Sean's initial thinking could be expanded. Importantly, they took turns exploring and ranking all five fee areas from Kepler's point of view, which helped them clarify their own interests and mandate as well. Based on their analysis, Sean realized that Bancroft and Kepler probably valued certain variables differently. He prepared to propose options for each issue area that would satisfy Bancroft's most important interests very well while still meeting Kepler's interests. Further, he bundled the options into multiple potential packages; he hoped that this would help to draw out Kepler's real preferences and might avoid positional anchoring around a single proposal.

Sean also began sharing his thinking with Bancroft client finance and senior executives to make sure that he had accurately understood his own organization's interests, to share initial thinking about options and packages, and to expand his license to invent more options at the table. Eager to avoid last year's mistakes, he also determined to dedicate as much time during the negotiation as he could to sharing and exploring Kepler's interests. Sean described himself to a colleague as feeling "better prepared for the negotiation than ever before, ready to ask lots of questions, and willing to listen."

Two days prior to the meeting, Sean contacted his negotiating partner Andy Feltner, Bancroft's client leader for Asia. Andy was taken aback by Sean's new plan but did his best to grasp it during a short cell-phone conversation. By now, both Sean and Andy had heard about Kepler renegotiations with other EMR agencies: Kepler was clearly taking an aggressive stance, and the new head of marketing procurement was apparently out to make a name for himself. Andy questioned the wisdom of trying out a new approach at such a critical moment, but acquiesced on the basis of the bleak reports from other EMR agencies and Sean's enthusiasm.

The day finally arrived. Sean and Andy rendezvoused in the Atlanta airport and spent their flight reviewing Sean's data and guidelines. Despite continued misgivings, Andy bought into the approach and the roles that he and Sean would play: Andy, soft-spoken, would focus on supporting the relationship while Sean would be the firm but fair no-

nonsense businessman. As he would later report, Sean worried about his ability to "really behave in a mutual gains way and remember all the questioning and listening techniques" when the negotiations actually began, yet he was excited by the prospects of a positive discussion with the client.

According to plan, Sean opened the meeting by reviewing the added value and increased efficiencies that Bancroft had produced that year, followed by the first of several package proposals he had prepared—one in which two variables were proposed to increase while three remained constant. The Kepler team listened, asked questions, and quickly made a counterproposal of their own: all five variables decrease or no deal! In previous negotiations—and especially during last year's—this would have signaled the beginning of the usual defensive haggling. Instead, Sean thanked them for their input and began exploring Kepler's underlying interests by asking questions and presenting multiple packages. More than once he was tempted to respond to their positional bargaining in kind, but Andy, sensing Sean's impatience, coolly picked up the conversation or requested short breaks to regroup.

Sean and Andy voluntarily shared Bancroft's key interests, including maintaining their overhead rate and preserving the opportunity to earn additional fees if performance criteria were met. Sensing a difference in Sean and Andy's approach, the Kepler team gradually became more collaborative and also proposed and adapted several packages. Throughout the process, Sean helped the Kepler team develop arguments that they could take back to their leaders and provided ample opportunities for them to save face. Consequently, the Kepler team engaged their back table more smoothly and demonstrated greater flexibility than Sean had predicted or than had been the case with other EMR agencies.

After just four hours, the two sides reached agreement: three of the key variables would remain unchanged; one would increase; and one would decrease. In addition, Bancroft made several guarantees relative to the amount of savings, increased efficiencies and added value that they believed could be delivered, and in exchange secured an increase in one of the performance bonus bands. Bancroft secured the client for another twelve months, with projected revenues and margin similar to the previous year and with a strong chance of achieving an upside. Kepler was pleased to claim a sizeable savings thanks to their management of total client spend. Further, they were able to report greater agency accountability by moving more of the fee into a performance-based incentive, book the efficiency improvement guarantee, and anticipate other savings from Bancroft's effective procurement of Kepler's third-party spending.

Sean and Andy felt confident that the deal they achieved would please both parties, as indeed it did: senior executives at both Kepler and Bancroft expressed their satisfaction with both the outcome and the process. Sean described the experience as "by far the most enjoyable and productive negotiation with Kepler I've had," though he added that the next time he would "do even more preparation . . . and engage Andy much earlier in the process."

This is the kind of case we like to hear about, of course. It contains specific new and different moves that were made (with some positive results) as well as lessons about what to do differently next time (start preparing earlier!). In our experience positive results are not uncommon when organizations augment training with interventions that create a more powerful context for change.

A predictable surprise in our work is this: even when substantial improvements are made and documented, everyone can slip back into bad habits very quickly. In chapter 5 we examine ways of measuring success more effectively and look at common barriers to sustaining negotiation improvements over the long term.

[5]

SUSTAIN YOUR NEW
COMPETITIVE ADVANTAGE

THE STEPS AND TASKS we've described thus far are necessary but not sufficient ingredients for building a world-class
negotiating organization. It takes a serious effort to diagnose and
remedy organizational shortcomings at a systemic level. Having
gone this far, it will be tempting for champions and sponsors to
find examples of success, declare victory, and move on to other
things. It is all too easy to assume that the improvements and
changes made by the organization will sustain themselves over
time. But as any physician will avow, monitoring gains and looking for early signs of relapse in the patient are an essential part of
treatment. So, too, it goes for organizations. Too often events are
held, glowing evaluation forms are returned, and a few successes
are held up as evidence of a positive return on investment. As we
discussed in chapter 4, holding up examples of successful experimentation is a critical champion task during the intervention
phase. But once new ways of doing things have been established,
champions must take charge of measuring outcomes more systematically and deeply.

This means taking the time to monitor progress and formulate ways of dealing with barriers or misalignments that may exist, and it means ensuring that adequate organizational resources are in place to continue with periodic training, coaching, and knowledge management. Such a commitment need not consume significant amounts of time or money; but measuring impacts and addressing persistent barriers is critical to detecting new or emerging problems and protecting long-term returns on investment. The first step is ensuring that the success criteria identified at the assessment phase are measured with sufficient care.

STEP 8: EVALUATE LEVEL IV—IMPACT

In 1959 Donald L. Kirkpatrick, a professor at the University of Wisconsin, published a series of articles in the *U.S. Training and Development Journal*, in which he suggested that training evaluation could occur at four levels: reaction, learning, behavior change, and impact (see table 5-1).[1] (To Kirkpatrick's four levels Jack

TABLE 5-1

Kirkpatrick's four levels

	What is measured	Advantages	Challenges
Level I	Reaction of participants	Easy to do	May not predict anything useful on the job
Level II	Learning (knowledge transfer)	Provides evidence that participants have learned	Not easy to measure complex learning or attitude change
Level III	Behavior change	Shows that training has produced change in how participants behave	Hard to measure actual behavior change; self-report may not be accurate
Level IV	Business results	Demonstrates organizational results of behavior change	Difficult to prove that impacts are due solely to one intervention

Source: Adapted from D. L. Kirkpatrick, *Evaluating Training Programs: The Four Levels* (San Francisco, CA: Berrett-Koehler, 1994).

Phillips and others added a fifth level, return on investment, or the sum of impacts minus the cost of the training/intervening. We see this fifth level as a derivative of the fourth level rather than a fundamentally new category.)[2] Most training programs, Kirkpatrick suggested, relied on Level I evaluation—the reaction of trainees to the training. Recent data suggests that 74 percent of training programs in the United States still rely solely on Level I evaluations to measure success.[3] In our view this is a mistake.

Perhaps we should not be surprised there are very few published studies linking negotiation training to Level IV results. Our research uncovered only one study (by Ferdinand Tesoro in 1998, involving Dell Computer sales staff) in which a negotiation training program's ROI was measured in terms of dollar gains, compared with a control group within the organization.[4] Another study (in 2001 by Peter Coleman and Ying Yong Joanne Lim), measured behavior change after an academic course, as judged by work peers and friends of participants.[5] While meta-analyses suggest that training as a whole can be effective, there has to date been very little measurement of the Level III and Level IV effects of *negotiation* training.[6]

It is easy to lay the blame at the feet of human resources and organizational development professionals, particularly those who are charged with demonstrating the value of their own spending and investment. But as globalization produces intense competitive pressure on organizations, those same professionals have often been the first to be let go when cost-cutting measures are required. Often HR professionals are measured by short-term, nuts-and-bolts metrics, like numbers of trainees per quarter and cost per trainee. (We'll have more to say about competitiveness and success metrics a little later.) It is not easy for organizations to measure the impact of new initiatives because change in both markets and organizations is continuous and therefore it is not always clear whether better results can be uniquely attributed to any one intervention.

How can champions and human resource or learning development staff—who are often overworked already—assess and underscore the impact of organizational interventions? The first step is to commit to gathering and evaluating data.

Gather Stories

Gathering preliminary data about the effectiveness of new resources or interventions need not be laborious and time-consuming. As described in earlier chapters, we routinely send out a simple e-mail to participants. We generally ask three questions:

1. Have you or your team tried anything different since the training event (or other intervention)?

2. If you have, what has the impact been (financially, legally, with respect to the negotiation process, risk management, and relationships, or other measures)?

3. If not, why not? What got in the way?

We are interested in learning about both changes and barriers to change. Sometimes we will ask whether participants have spent more time on key behaviors (such as "thought more about the other side's BATNA") as a way of reminding participants of them and for the purpose of aggregating results more quantitatively. For example, after a global training event for senior leaders from across its training companies, WPP champions sent out an e-mail to participants asking how many had adopted the core behaviors of the mutual gains approach, and what the perceived impact of these changes was. The format of the survey allowed WPP to first assess how many participants reported trying specific new behaviors, by showing percentages of the number of people who said they had tried each behavior. We learned that, on the high end, 95 percent had thought more about the other side's interests and perceived alternatives prior to negotiating; 84 percent had spent more time thinking about their own BATNA; 74 percent spent more time listening for interests during the negotiation. On the low end, only 5 percent had tried using a contingent agreement in the final contract. This kind of feedback leads us to be curious about *why* some behaviors are not being tried. Is it that participants have not kept them in mind? That no situations have arisen in which they could be deployed? Are they viewed as irrelevant? Too difficult to manage? Blocked by others in the organization? Discouraged by current incentives? The point of inquiring is to learn what ought to be done to provide further assistance, advice, or training.

In addition, the WPP survey asked participants to describe in a few sentences the effects of their training on their client negotiations. A sample of actual responses from one tailored training program included:

- "It's made me fundamentally rethink our approach to negotiation preparation."

- "By far the most enjoyable and productive negotiation with [client] that I've ever done."

- "One client's income has gone up by 42 percent, not all because of the MGA, but it certainly helped."

- "I have just negotiated the best music deal that [client] has ever struck and it's largely down to applying the MGA."

On the other hand, some responses suggested that new practices were either being blocked by others in the organization, or were not leading to results that were discernibly different.

But surveys are not enough. It is critical to follow up with brief confidential interviews. Why? First, measurement experts would quibble that *perceived* impacts are not the same as *actual* impacts. It is important to ask participants how they've determined the impact, to make sure that they're not simply "fluffing" the results. Second, very often the *stories* behind these brief responses are much more compelling than brief feedback might suggest, sometimes because the trainee had not thought of a way to measure the impact. A new process that a team uses to prepare more effectively, or a new idea for creating value; a new way of approaching client concerns—these can become competitive advantages that should be propagated across the organization. Taking the time to draw them out is well worth the effort. Finally, it is important to follow up in a nonthreatening and confidential way with those participants who have not tried new "moves" or who have not met with success. It is critical to elicit barriers to change that might require rethinking or improving the intervention; or making other organizational changes.

For example, Hewlett-Packard's Global Contracts team (described in chapter 4) was created in part after HP discovered that training alone was not sufficient. A follow-up after what had seemed like breakthrough training sessions revealed that while procurement managers saw great merit in adopting a mutual gains approach, they felt constrained by the legal language handed down by general counsel once specifications, price, and deliverables had been agreed. This "required language" produced positional bargaining at the very end of the negotiation with suppliers and discouraged efforts to problem-solve legal disagreements between suppliers and partners. In response, we encouraged negotiation champion Ben Webster to explain the problem to his vice president. Once she understood the nature of the problem, she created the Global Contracts team, made up of legal and business-line representatives, who then *prepared together* for negotiations, considering interests and options from both the internal client and legal perspectives. This meant that the team members from Legal had to clarify their mandate with the general counsel, which in turn led to tailored training from their own leaders that focused on ways of using legal language more flexibly and responsively while protecting the company from certain risks. At the risk of stating the obvious, going back to the procurement group with advanced training was not going to produce the kind of organizational changes—in terms of roles, mandate, and authority—that was required.

Taking the time to seek meaningful feedback provides opportunities for conversation that can lead to much more meaningful

Potential Impacts of Level III Changes

We find that it can help to list the kinds of impacts that might potentially occur as a result of Level III (behavioral) changes. A sample list might include the following kinds of impacts:

- Cost savings for our organization (short- or longer-term)

- Cost savings for our counterparts that can be shared with us

- Cost of negotiating (time, personnel) reduced

- Sales/revenue increase (immediate, future)

- Improvement in quality of goods/services

- Quality of service/product enables new capabilities (innovation)

- Agreement incorporates more effective performance incentives

- Faster turnaround on key deliverables or support

- Risk management—decrease our maximum liability

- Risk management—decrease likelihood of risky event

- Risk management—turnover reduced via higher morale

- Agreement lengthened (income stabilized; investments enabled)

- New or potential work or markets uncovered

- Agreement will be easier to implement

- Agreement more durable, robust (via contingent agreements, e.g.)

- Agreement includes process/operational improvements

- Better alignment of roles, accountabilities

- Trust among parties has been improved

- Brand/reputation has been protected or enhanced

- Improved communication/responsiveness among implementing parties

information, evaluation, and subsequent intervention than surveys alone. (See "Potential Impacts of Level III Changes" for some of the issues that might be surfaced during these feedback sessions.)

Develop Quantitative Estimates

Once participants have been surveyed about new behaviors (Level III) and at least a sample of individuals and/or teams interviewed to uncover more meaningful information, it is important to be able to produce for the sponsors(s) some *estimate* of Level IV impact. For example, McDonald's asks all general managers and vice presidents in our workshops to think of recent negotiations and imagine upcoming ones. They're asked to estimate the annual gains they expect as a result of the workshop. When the training has been tailored effectively to address the contexts and issues that participants face and includes a specific process model, it is not a leap for trainees to imagine doing one or two things differently and estimate how future interactions will be affected. In some cases the estimated impact can run into millions of dollars per trainee. Although they are not bottom-line measurements, such estimates provide important information from those in the trenches about whether the training efforts seem likely to produce tangible change in both behavior and results.

More Level IV-type information is also gathered through our routine follow-up e-mail to all workshop participants. We are often able to collect stories of success with numbers attached ("I saved $250,000 in one deal alone because I thought more about their BATNA"). In other cases, we are able to document barriers to implementation ("Others in my department need to become familiar with this approach before my team can deploy it effectively" or "I haven't been able to renegotiate my mandate in a way that would allow me to create more value"). Surfacing these barriers is just as important as documenting impacts.

Aggregating survey results is one way to provide estimates of impact. Simply adding up the gains reported by each person over a period of months or quarters and dividing by number of participants can produce a per capita gain measure (which, after subtracting the direct and indirect costs of the training or intervention, yields an ROI estimate). Yet we want to reemphasize that, while better than nothing, surveys completed quickly by time-starved executives may be poor measures. People cannot always recall complex events in detail, or correlate them with discrete questions. Interviewing six to ten participants for twenty minutes and asking them to describe a negotiation often leads to new insights and realizations, and directs attention to more subtle changes, impacts, or barriers, than would have been described in a survey.

Organizations that have created a virtual center of excellence (described in chapter 4) have the benefit of an interactive online forum to draw out information through inquiries and posts. Participants can read what has already been posted in response to a question. On the positive side, this helps participants to note and respond to, or elaborate on, things they had not freely recalled. On the negative side, participants who are pressed for time often simply respond with a simple "ditto" or "not sure I agree" or some other response that does not deepen anyone's insight about their experience.

Some of these measures are harder to translate into short-term, bottom-line improvements than others. We don't deny the importance of financial metrics in measuring success. But long-term success depends on a larger set of factors that are often harder to monetize with confidence.

When we first worked with HP, the company's negotiation success metrics were focused on reducing cost and consolidating spending. We provided tailored training to procurement managers entrusted with purchasing $14 billion annually in "indirect" goods (company cars, energy, real estate) and services (travel, legal, consulting, marketing, etc.). One of the problems that emerged during assessment was that procurement represented many business groups across the company with diverse interests and preferences. In addition, they were accountable to the CFO, and to legal advisers who were focused primarily on eight legal terms and conditions (and rarely on the business and delivery terms). Procurement was accountable to all of these groups.

Savings were closely tracked at the organizational level, but the degree to which a deal achieved other key organization deliverables was not included in deal description/evaluation. Because of the misalignment between procurement's incentives and the interests of the organization as a whole, business leaders sometimes lost their preferred suppliers and didn't understand why; in other cases, legal advisers held up deals for months that appeared to expose the company to what they considered to be unacceptable risk. Stakeholders (other than the procurement managers) were unaware of the needs of other stakeholders in the system; instead, they blamed procurement when the outcome didn't meet their aspirations, or when the deal was delayed.

Moreover, the key signatories (business and procurement vice presidents), who were ultimately responsible for the deal, were often presented with hundred-page documents with few guidelines about what made the deal better or worse than past deals. Having been uninvolved until the final document arrived on their desks, they were faced with the choice of either holding up the deal or rubber-stamping it without fully understanding the interests, alternatives, and trade-offs that had generated it.

Working with Ben Webster, we looked at the current negotiation process, which was highly linear (a sequence of forms, conversations, and approvals) and did not adequately involve key stakeholders early enough in the process. Webster was able to recruit sponsors several levels up who understood that the system needed fixing. With some coaching from us, the Indirect Procurement team grafted the mutual gains approach onto their existing requirements and constraints, creating a new and unique HP process. This process involved earlier and more focused conversations and forms that required negotiators—together with their stakeholders—to explicitly evaluate and improve alternatives, understand and rank their varying interests, create options, and gather market data and benchmarks. Having a clear plan provided the negotiators with more freedom to invent options at the table and gave the executives an opportunity to influence the deal at the front end, increasing the likelihood of later acceptance.

The goal of HP's negotiation framework, which crystallized during these changes and was endorsed at the highest levels of the company, was to create and secure value. To ensure this outcome, Webster helped the group to spell out more explicit success criteria that would drive the best overall deal for HP. The proposed criteria fell into four categories: financial success, operational excellence (process efficiency), risk management, and relationships (see figure 5-1).

"All these things matter to HP, but it was critical to help everyone understand that stakeholders inside the company value

FIGURE 5-1

Proposed deal-level metrics, HP

Financial success

Cost reduction*
(annual value)

Cost avoidance*
(annual value)

Execution: Actual versus plan
Forecast versus final contracted rate

Operational excellence

Contract cycle time*
(from negotiation plan approval to contract signature)

Total cost to negotiate*
Labor (FTE) + travel + deal-specific data cost

Relationships

HP
Survey score/basket

Supplier
Survey score/basket

Utilize sales/alliance/channel partner tools for tracking relationships

Risk management

Improvement on Big 8 legal policies*

Approved negotiation plan in place*

*Linked to business unit-level metrics.

them differently," Webster noted. The procurement team had been divided in ways that reflected the differing interests of stakeholders, including legal staff and various business stakeholders. The new preparation and endorsement process required stakeholders to work together and linked their individual success to the "overall success of the deal," rather than to their legal or business-linked managers and stakeholders.

Financial success metrics included year-over-year savings (adjusted for inflation), and cost avoidance—measures taken to reduce additional costs in view of increasing market benchmarks and in view of the quality of (sometimes poor) BATNAs. With respect to operational excellence, HP was able to improve the average time-to-contract from twelve weeks to four weeks. HP began to measure internal customer satisfaction to assess how well the agreements met core business goals and also evaluated whether supplier consolidation had been achieved in a manner consistent with sound supplier management strategy.

Finally, risk management metrics included reducing exposure to legal risks, evaluation of quality control improvements, and comparisons to relevant current and past agreements. At the time of this writing, steps to measure the health of relationships with counterparts were still to be implemented, but had been included as a part of the phased change progress.

Share the Good News

As a result of gathering informal stories about moves that participants have made at the table, or ways they have prepared differently, we are able to provide feedback, both positive and negative, about how people have tried to move forward and what has happened as a result. Describing even small wins has an important effect. In cases where it appears that a major win or a particularly ingenuous application was involved, a champion or outside consultant can be assigned to interview the negotiator on a confidential basis to pull out the larger story. In cases where the negotiator is concerned about confidentiality, the actual details can be disguised (changing sectors or products) while preserving the actual application. In cases where counterparts can be involved, an even richer profile of the negotiation can be generated, one that describes the relationship from both sides and reviews how it was enhanced or protected.

It is important for leadership and sponsors to reward efforts, even those that fail. This can be done by distributing an article in which leaders comment on and endorse the efforts made by negotiators, and external experts can comment on the case—either describing why the efforts produced a benefit, or other strategies the negotiator might have tried if they did not. If participants do not see a clear benefit to changing, and also see clear risks, it is unrealistic to expect them to change. Therefore, even in cases where a superior outcome has not been immediately apparent, the connection of new behaviors to core organizational values and clearly understood success criteria is an important step.

Balance Short- and Long-Term Gains

As mentioned earlier, we believe that effective leaders must direct the attention of their organizations evenly between short- and long-term gains, in view of both opportunities and threats. It is not enough to estimate short-term gains and losses. If a negotiation produces short-term gains at the expense of long-term relationships or opportunities for innovation, growth, or cost-reduction, then value (as measured by longer-term metrics) is actually being destroyed. Examples of short-termism in corporate management abound.

One example of short-term gains at the expense of long-term ones arose in our work with a global manufacturer. Under pressure to manage costs, this company pushed its supplier, which made a highly customized part, to accept price reductions—with no effort to create value as part of the package. The disgruntled supplier took active steps to diversify its client portfolio. When the manufacturer experienced a sudden and unexpected upsurge in demand for one of its highly customized new products, it went to the supplier and requested an increase in production. The supplier, with (perhaps disingenuous) apologies, effectively said, "Sorry, we can't. We've got too much business from other sources right now." The cost to the manufacturer in lost sales ran into tens of millions of dollars. When we uncovered this story, it was clear that the manufacturer had not found a way to learn from it. Instead, the supplier was blamed, and no real steps to change negotiation strategy were taken. The company had failed to understand how a strategy of exacting price reductions, without engaging in any additional value creation efforts with the supplier, had worsened the relationship and dramatically increased business risk.

Fortunately, that company now has a scorecard that includes risk management, including the state of operational and business relationships, as a key metric for assessing the success of critical agreements. As we noted in the introduction, a successful negotiation:

1. Produces an outcome that is better for all parties than their respective no-agreement alternatives

2. Uses a process that is efficient in terms of time and resources

3. Maximizes the chances that the parties find and exploit differences in their interests to produce joint gains

4. Generates a contract that is understandable and likely to be implemented effectively

5. Manages risks associated with brand and reputation

6. Makes future dealings easier

7. Reflects the values of the organization

In this case the organization realized it had relied too heavily on measuring and rewarding the first criterion, at the expense of several others (notably items 3–7).

Learn from Failures

As Woody Allen has famously noted, "If you're not failing every now and again, it's a sign you're not doing anything very innovative." Although we don't expect companies to actively seek to fail, we do believe that successful companies have at least two overarching strengths: a willingness and capacity to "confront the brutal facts" (as Jim Collins and his colleagues describe in their best-seller *Good-to-Great*), and a willingness and capacity to change.[7] Together, these constitute a critical competitive advantage. Capacity to change depends on the capacity to confront difficult truths: if companies ignore or gloss over failures, attributing them to external factors (the other side, market conditions, new technologies, weather, etc.), they miss key opportunities to improve performance, seize opportunities, and avoid losses.

To confront brutal truths about negotiation performance, two things are required: time spent *collecting information* and reflecting on its meaning, and an insightful and candid *diagnosis*, often with the help of someone from outside the operating system, about what could have been done more effectively. Investing time can be as simple as setting aside thirty to sixty minutes each month to reflect on a particular negotiation, glean key lessons, share them, and capture comments and feedback. Who should be part of the effort? If the negotiation involved a team, it is often helpful to bring that group together to think about how it worked together; what happened in the negotiation; and what might have been more effective in terms of preparation, value creation, and distribution, and dealing with predictable surprises. If the team and its leader(s) are able to have a candid conversation, such meetings can be very useful. For individuals, it can be helpful to convene on a semiregular basis a group of negotiators in the organization who share an interest in improving their skills and processes. This kind of *learning community* can bring together people from different departments and divisions to talk about negotiations, both generally and in terms of recent cases. Again, a virtual center of excellence can provide a ready-made platform for these efforts.

In some instances it can be helpful to disguise the actual names and details in cases that have been collected, presenting them as generically as possible and asking leadership to evaluate how well the negotiators did. This exercise can be immensely useful for both the presenter and the group because it focuses evaluators on the problems and behaviors, rather than on the department or individuals involved. But in other cases, where leadership does not yet have a good understanding of negotiation theory or where there may be issues of trust, having an outside negotiation expert review the cases and offer a diagnostic response and recommendations is likely to be more effective.

No change or learning initiative should be considered a complete success unless it can be shown to impact metrics that matter to the organization. It is not enough to collect post-training surveys that ask how people felt about the training. Changing negotiation behaviors requires a commitment to measuring both behavior change and the impact of that change. It requires gathering stories that can be shared with, and analyzed by, others in the organization. It requires developing quantitative estimates of impacts and potential impacts, translating "softer" but critical factors (e.g., relationships and brand) into probabilistic estimates of value and risk. It requires putting in place communication and learning processes that enable those who have been through training to continue to learn. And it requires a commitment to measuring gains across both shorter and longer time frames. Finally, it requires a willingness to confront failure and to remain curious about its sources. It is to this topic that we now turn.

STEP 9: ADDRESS PERSISTENT BARRIERS

In a highly mobile and rapidly changing world, organizations and their leaders should anticipate persistent barriers to sustaining the structures and processes necessary to support effective negotiations. Confronting barriers requires both curiosity and resolve—curiosity because there are no simple diagnoses or prescriptions at this stage, and resolve because it is all too easy to decide that only so much time can be spent on one initiative before the next one demands attention. Going this far and then stopping, however, might be compared to building a house and then not weatherproofing the roof and walls adequately. Unless there is a commitment to actively sustain the gains made at earlier stages, the organization's investment in organizational capability can be wasted. The good news is that the commitment can be modest if done properly. For many of the common persistent problems (see "Seven Barriers to Implementing a Mutual Gains Approach") there are remedies, although as always, context matters. This section provides some overarching prescriptions for dealing with these problems.

Assume Rational Conduct

Whenever desired change does not follow efforts to spur it, or when individuals or groups are found to be lapsing back to old habits, it is easy to simply attribute the persistence of old behaviors to some intrinsic deficiency in a person or group. "Some people just don't get it," you might hear. Or, "that guy has always been out for himself." One of our favorites: "These guys are engineers; what do you expect?" But in our view, there are usually good reasons for bad habits.

When examples of old behaviors arise, it will be tempting for champions who have put time and effort into improving negotiation processes and models to resort to reprimanding individuals or groups who fail to adopt or maintain best practices, or to blaming individuals or teams for being selfish or incompetent. It will also be tempting, in some cases, to send out harsh e-mails or memos. But yielding to such temptations is a mistake because it misses an opportunity to understand perceptions, feelings, attitudes, and behaviors—and their causes. Beating people over the head only

Seven Barriers to Implementing a Mutual Gains Approach

These are seven of the most common and persistent barriers to implementing a mutual gains or value-creating approach to negotiation:

- Turnover, reductions, or growth/mobility in the organization lead to lost knowledge and skills.

- Learning opportunities go missed because employees are reluctant to share failures (or to share successes in cases where other organizations or clients are involved).

- New business processes, roles, or teams emerge that conflict or compete at a tactical level with the steps required for negotiation success.

- Some groups in the organization refuse to work within the new framework, either because the new approach appears to disadvantage them or because their immediate goals and incentives are not aligned with the organization's overall goals.

- Champions and sponsors turn their attention to other things and are not replaced.

- Leadership trumps its own endorsement by reverting to short-term metrics that thwart the creation of long-term value and preservation of relationships.

- The strategic/competitive environment presents genuinely few opportunities for crafting integrative agreements.

leads to defensiveness and pushback. Understanding what is preventing progress allows champions and organizations to diagnose underlying problems and to formulate effective interventions.

Rather than repeatedly pushing the new approach, it is more effective to work hard to cultivate a sense of curiosity. Curiosity invariably leads to inquiry. How does the individual or group view process alternatives, costs, and benefits? How can their underlying assumptions and interests be treated as additional information that can lead to improved prescriptions? As Chris Argyris and others have shown, inquiring in order to surface "theories-in-use" (what people's actions seem to indicate as contrasted with their stated or "espoused theories") is a much more effective path. Inquiry can help distinguish whether the problems reflect a lack of awareness or capability, or a lack of motivation or intention.

Use Confidential Interviewing

Persistent barriers to implementing organizational practices can fall into three diagnostic buckets: *can't, shouldn't,* and *won't.*

Can't *barriers*

In organizations where growth and/or turnover are high, new managers *can't* do what is required; they simply lack the knowledge or skills. In some cases, particularly in industries with high turnover employees may not be aware of the negotiation model, concepts, and tools that we have described. Negotiators and those who support them may fail to assess what is required in terms of preparation, or understand how success will be measured and rewarded. They may not have insight into what is possible in terms of value creation at the table. They may not have access to data or know how to interpret available information in ways that support an advantageous distribution of the value that is created. Moreover, even when individuals have attended a workshop, applying new skills in a complex context requires the organizational support and learning opportunities we have described. In particular, to the degree that negotiations involve multiple departments and/or technical knowledge, organizations should not assume that trained individuals will be able to invent options for mutual gain all by themselves.[8] Organization benefit by leveraging the thinking of experienced and talented negotiators in these situations.

And that's the good news: to a significant degree, *can't* problems are tractable. Addressing them requires three things:

1. Confidential interviewing to assess the extent and nature of the problem, without retribution

2. An organizational culture in which asking for help is rewarded, or at least not punished

3. Assistance that is tailored to the group's needs—training, individual and group coaching (particularly around preparation), and resource support from a center of excellence

For those new to the organization or to negotiation, it is particularly important to see examples of how to apply the model. This includes stories about *victories* (in terms of improved outcomes, better processes, lowered risks, and protected or enhanced relationships) and *worst nightmares* (in terms of past failures and lessons learned). Showing people what the approach sounds like in their own context is a powerful learning tool. As Janice Nadler and her colleagues have shown through clever experiments, individuals who see others effectively create value in a negotiation go on to achieve better outcomes themselves than negotiators who are given more information. (Although interestingly, they can't always explain what they did differently as a result of having seen the example.)[9] Showing people what works in a particular context, and what it looks and sounds like, is important. This is why we believe so strongly that organizations ought to build their own specific resource centers to address the kinds of negotiations their people are most likely to face.

Shouldn't *barriers*

A second and more difficult kind of barrier can take the form of an individual or operating group ambivalent about implementing some or all of the new approach. For various reasons they have a sense that they *shouldn't* implement the approach. This might be because the gains from using the approach are not immediately clear; because a new or unfamiliar approach appears to expose them or their group to higher risk or scrutiny; or because new processes might provoke conflict over roles or authority or in some other way create problems within the organization or with negotiation partners.

In some cases, the benefits of applying a new approach may not be sufficiently clear to all stakeholders. "We've always done it this way and it has worked well enough," is the kind of comment that emerges. This can be the case even when champions and sponsors have been diligent in their efforts to introduce new approaches and interventions have produced significant improvements in negotiated outcomes and processes. In a world where time is short and attention is difficult to sustain, it is rational to assume that people will pursue paths that lead to the biggest perceived gains and/or minimize losses and risks. If taking more time to prepare, for example, appears to be a time sink that does not lead to reasonably immediate rewards (including reinforcement for having been more diligent), then it is predictable and rational for people to choose not to maintain the effort and diligence.

Consider an example. We worked with an automaker customer care group whose job involved handling customer complaints and making sure customers were left feeling well-treated. Each customer care representative had a budget limit for dealing with most problems. Performance was measured largely in terms of the happiness of the customer. Small wonder then that the company found that most complainants ended up being offered the maximum cash reimbursement without much negotiation.

To recall our three measures of success, the representatives were rewarded for maintaining the relationship and for doing so in a time-efficient way. There was no reward, however, for achieving a better outcome for the company (in terms of dollars saved). Training the representatives to negotiate more effectively was not likely to generate improved negotiations *unless* success was measured and rewarded differently; for example, the representatives could have been rewarded each quarter based on a weighted average of their customer satisfaction metrics and the money spent/saved in each case.

Won't *barriers*

The third kind of barrier—and often the hardest to surface and remedy—is the *won't* barrier. Notwithstanding exhortations from the organization's leaders to pull together for the common good or do what's best for the organization, individuals and groups in different organizational functions often possess interests, incentives, and alternatives to agreement that diverge in some way from the organization's overall goals. We call the conflicts that can result *strategic conflicts*, because successful organizations must simultaneously pursue different strategic goals (growth, margins, reputation, quality, risk management, customer experience, and so forth) and in so doing, typically create different salient goals and incentives across functions.

For example, a sales representative knows she will be rewarded with a large bonus for bringing in a new account. She makes commitments or otherwise agrees to a deal that secures her a large bonus in the short run, but leads to a poor or unnecessarily risky deal for the organization over the long term.

In other cases negotiators may perceive that using MGA would require preparing collaboratively with others in the organization; and if the negotiators would rather not deal with those people, they avoid preparing effectively. At Hewlett-Packard, preparation habits were slow to change until the procurement leadership *required* a preparation form to be completed and signed in advance of key negotiations. Once this happened and managers saw the results of such efforts—in terms of increased collaboration, increased access to (and concern from) leadership, and increased clarity about how leadership really ranked the company's competing interests—the benefits were clear.

Another example: an engineer leader refuses to agree to modifications in a product design that the VP of marketing insists are critical for growing customer share. Why? It turns out that the engineering group is responsible for quality assurance and the proposed changes would likely disrupt a process that has taken them years to perfect. Moreover, their leader is new to the job and fears that his team will resent and see him as weak if he "caves in" to demands from marketing. The group's job will get more difficult, and he will be blamed if the changes fail to meet quality specifications. To him, the prospective gains from working with Marketing look marginal whereas the cost looks large.

Foster Candid Feedback

Another way to address persistent problems is to share them and ask for suggestions. This can be done by posting a problem or issue on a Web discussion forum, sending out an electronic survey, or using other virtual learning and communication tools. Allowing people anonymity in such forums often permits the sharing of problems that would be too sensitive to bring up in face-to-face interviews. And it can sometimes lead to surprisingly good suggestions for what to try next.

In cases where trust is low or people have felt exposed or blamed, it is useful to construct a hypothetical case in which things work well, and another one in which they do not. Describing barriers in another industry that nonetheless has similar organizational themes or challenges can spur input and discussion from employees or partners who might otherwise not want to respond. We've seen rooms full of leaders "unlock" into high-stakes disclosure and discussion when the case at hand does not directly involve them, but involves the same kinds of issues, problems, and barriers they face in their own organization.

Recognize and Mitigate Impacts

It is important that consulted parties understand the product of the interviewing process. In cases where incentives are misaligned, it is critical to align them without adversely affecting those employees who have been candid. Those whose candor is used to worsen their situation or increase their workload cannot be expected to be candid in future interviews. If incentives are changed, those affected must feel that the new design is both sensible and fundamentally fair. If, for example, sales commissions are made a function of both upfront revenue *and* value creation during implementation (keeping operational costs lower throughout the agreement, for example), then the total package should be as attractive to the sales force.

There are tangible interests that underlie and maintain bad old habits. Chief among these are financial reward and workload reduction. But there are also psychological interests that can be compelling. "Change around here is so rapid and continuous that many people in my division just want to stay under the radar," one executive told us. Psychological interests can include feeling competent (by sticking with what one knows); avoiding scrutiny or evaluation; avoiding risk of failure; feeling indispensable in a crisis; and working with people one likes. Yet it is stressful for most people to live with the tension that is raised by misalignment and the secrecy or dissembling that usually accompanies it.

In short, most people are willing to change if they feel they will not be blamed or exposed, and if they can see a possible future arrangement that does not significantly worsen their own outcomes. It is therefore important for leaders to solicit and monitor feedback from groups whose business processes stand to change from implementing a mutual gains framework.

For example, we worked with a negotiation team in a technology company whose leader fully endorsed value creation as the group's focus. Yet the group's bonuses remained yoked to quarterly and yearly savings targets, which were measured (very narrowly) in terms of upfront spend. Not surprisingly, the group quickly decided that a more comprehensive notion of value creation was not going to be rewarded. The leader blamed the failure to change on the group's collective lack of creativity and skill. We saw it differently.

In cases where stakeholders are reluctant to admit they have private but important interests (such as not taking on additional responsibilities), asking them what they think drives their colleagues in other roles may reveal key insights. Psychologists have found that members of Western cultures are particularly likely to harbor unrealistically positive self-evaluations. In one study, for example, medical residents were asked how likely it was that their prescriptive judgment had been influenced by visits and perks from pharmaceutical companies. While 61 percent said they had not been affected, 84 percent reported that their colleagues' judgment had been affected.[10] A similar dynamic can occur inside organizations. Thus, asking people what they see others thinking, feeling, believing, and doing is often a good way to elicit concerns and interests that need to be addressed before adoption of new processes can occur.

Work to Preserve Trust

Finally, largely because preparation is so central to the mutual gains approach, building world-class negotiating practices requires sustaining collaboration across groups. In competitive environments it is all too easy to lose the trust of others (often without realizing it). Distrust can arise because of failure to live up to commitments, because one party feels another does not have necessary competence or judgment, or because one party or group feels that others are "out for themselves" and will exploit information or efforts that are extended. In one organization, key product developers did not trust the sales force to give them enough time to improve an application. "They'll take whatever we say is possible and then give us half the time to do it right," said one. Consequently the product developers suggested to the sales force that some new features were simply not possible to create. Obviously, this kind of distrust leads to lost opportunities and can pose a risk to continuing competitiveness.

Maintaining trust is a particularly salient issue for both leaders and negotiators. As organizations grow in size and complexity, it becomes less possible to explain how problems were perceived, how options were generated, and how decisions or actions were selected from among the options. All that is perceived is the outcome, and to the degree that those affected feel that the outcome was in some way unwise or unfair, the absence of careful explanation creates a void into which attributions can rush. We often see examples of the *fundamental attribution error*, whereby managers ascribe traits or motives to others (both positive and negative) based on proposals, decisions, or actions. In environments where conflict is already high, attributions become particularly frequent and negative, as anyone who has been to a loud town hall meeting can attest.

Negotiators and leaders can reduce the likelihood of losing trust by making sure to repeatedly:

1. Clarify the decision rules, the decisions process, and the roles that different people will play in the process (e.g., who will make the decision, how others will be involved)

2. Describe the interests or goals that are driving proposed actions or decisions

3. Share data or analyses that support assumptions about alternatives, interests, constraints, and the fairness of how gains or losses are shared

4. Describe the principles or values that are consistent with the decision or action and acknowledge any possible perceived inconsistency between the action or decision with values or principles

5. Ask for comments and feedback and remain open to influence when better ideas are presented

---

Leading change is always difficult, and particularly when the change involves complex behaviors and systems. Building a world-class negotiating organization involves learning about what changes mean to individuals and groups, who may not know how to change (but are afraid to say this), who feel they should not change (because of possible risks or adverse consequences for partners inside or outside the organization), or who resist change because they see it as a threat to their current preferences or compensation. It is wise to assume that people have their reasons for not changing and to cultivate curiosity on the part of champions and consultants. It is best to create processes that protect confidentiality so that concerns are correctly identified. Effective leaders address rather than dismiss concerns, by providing additional assistance, or by clarifying goals and procedures, and/or realigning incentives so that change does not negatively impact employees in ways that had not been contemplated. Finally, providing a culture where trust flourishes catalyzes efforts to overcome and address resistance. Trust flourishes when leadership displays curiosity, concern, and candor. Leadership, perhaps more than anything else, is the secret ingredient that makes change successful.

Think Systemically

As should be clear by now, a key to sustaining the competitive advantage that comes from enhancing any organization's negotiating capabilities is to think systemically about change. We started out many pages ago by laying out a model for building a world-class negotiating organization. Figure 2-6, our earlier graphical representation of the process, was spare, a three-phase model involving nine steps. In the intervening chapters we've laid out those nine steps in more detail, providing prescriptive advice along the way. Our resulting model of the actions required to build a world-class negotiating organization is by now more elaborate (see figure 5-2), while remaining conceptually clear.

Although figure 5-2 shows a step-by-step model, we recognize that in many cases the course of change will involve recursive, parallel, and interdependent moves. Notwithstanding theories to

FIGURE 5-2

Creating a world-class negotiating organization

ASSESS current challenges and opportunities	**CREATE** a culture of learning	**SUSTAIN** your new competitive advantage

1 Start with a sound theory: The mutual gains approach
- Keep culture in mind
- Specify success criteria

2 Assess negotiation performance
- Use confidential interviewing
- Analyze the findings from multiple perspectives
- Highlight opportunities
- Avoid assigning blame

3 Make diagnoses and provide recommendations
- Diagnose gaps and opportunities
- Assess current learning strategies
- Provide a vision for the future

4 Identify sponsors and champions
- Start with a champion
- Secure senior leader sponsorship
- Create funding for intervention
- Commit to goals

5 Provide a common model and language
- Provide training to core leaders
- Tailor the training materials
- Provide new templates
- Encourage opportunistic experiments
- Provide effective coaching

6 Adjust and align operating procedures
- Pinpoint procedures that need to be changed
- Mandate a better negotiation preparation process
- Realign relevant incentives
- Clarify roles and responsibilities

7 Commit to organizational learning
- Support the champions
- Document successes (and failures)
- Create a virtual center of excellence
- Roll out additional training as needed

8 Evaluate (level IV) impact
- Gather stories
- Develop quantitative estimates
- Share the good news
- Balance short- and long-term gains
- Learn from failures

9 Address persistent barriers
- Assume rational conduct
- Use confidential interviewing
- Foster candid feedback
- Recognize and mitigate impacts
- Work to preserve trust
- Think systemically

the contrary, organizational change is rarely, if ever, linear. We provide a linear model for its heuristic value, but it should be clear that we are committed to a systemic model of change management. An organization or group should not throw up its hands if some steps initially look less tractable than others, or if they have moved ahead on some fronts (e.g., opportunistic experiments) but not on others.

For example, at WPP, there have been some groups and companies who have moved quickly to adopt MGA in their negotiations (both internal and with clients) and others who have not. Some groups have moved to create learning platforms, look at successes and failures by collecting cases studies, and changed the way that they prepare. Other groups, because of turnover or other reasons, have had difficulty in identifying champions to carry forward the necessary efforts and sponsors who have been willing to push for and encourage changes. To some degree, making progress requires moving opportunistically, but with a realistic appraisal of the risks that are incurred when steps are skipped. Thus, we advocate moving through the model in the way we have outlined, but we are cautiously optimistic that in some cases it is possible to make progress without rigidly adhering to a linear process.

STEP 10: LEAD FOR THE LONG TERM

Building a world-class negotiating organization can be made much easier when leaders are committed to building *long-term organizational value*, and when their actions and decisions reflected and demonstrated this commitment to everyone else in the organization. Throughout this book we've argued that, in effect, training courses that focus on skill building are not likely in and of themselves to produce meaningful organizational changes and improvements in negotiation. All nine steps—in three phases—are important. Yet the model is incomplete without a tenth component, which is perhaps less a step than an ethos: a commitment by leaders to focus on building value for the long term.

Organizations whose values, measures, and rewards reflect a commitment to the long term are the ones most likely to succeed in implementing a mutual gains approach, or any other approach that seeks to help the organization balance multiple goals and objectives in a complex world. It sounds simple, but as any CEO of a large company would be quick to report, creating long-term value while consistently producing sufficient value along the way is anything but simple. There are enormous pressures to produce or protect short-term profits or revenues in ways that often put long-term success at risk.

Some would argue that a long-term perspective is a fundamental aspect of what it means to lead. Warren Bennis wrote, "Leaders keep their eyes on the horizon—not just the bottom line."[11] Negotiation gurus David Lax and Jim Sebenius devote their efforts to helping organizations "create and claim value for the long term."[12] But we don't assume that organizational operations and decisions are always characterized by this tendency. Instead, our experience suggests that as complexity and competition in a global economy increase, a gap between long-term planning and short-term decisions and actions emerges. Negotiation is an arena in which this gap or dissociation emerges in tangible ways.

The Dilemma: "Win as Much as You Can"[13]

To understand this growing gap, consider an abstract exercise—one version of the most widely studied exercises in the world (the subject of thousands of studies by game theorists, economists, political scientists, and psychologists). Imagine four participants or "players" sitting at a card table. Each has in hand an X card and a Y card. Over ten "rounds" each participant simultaneously puts forward one of his or her two cards. The payoffs for each player are a function of the patterns of Xs and Ys that are put forward in that round (see table 5-2):

TABLE 5-2

"Win as much as you can"

X's	Y's	Payoffs
4	0	Each player loses $1
3	1	Each X wins $1 Y loses $3
2	2	Each X wins $2 Each Y loses $2
1	3	X wins $3 Each Y loses $1
0	4	Each player wins $1

Imagine further than these payouts increase in special temporary "bonus rounds" (rounds 5 and 8 and 10) by a factor of three (round 5) or five (round 8) or ten (round 10). Thus, for example, in round ten, an X played against three Ys would yield the X-player $30. Or, if all four played Y, each would win $10.

If you take these rules as given, and all four players play Y in every round, each wins $25 in the course of the game, and the total value created by all four players is $100. Yet very few groups in the thousands of experiments that have been run manage to generate $100. Why is this? There are at least three reasons, and we spell them out because we believe that this simple exercise and the results it generates actually have more complex but ubiquitous analogs in the real world.

First, the game is called "Win as Much as You Can." As Lee Ross and Andrew Ward showed in a series of brilliant experiments using a similar exercise, the name of the game can greatly affect how people behave, regardless of the payoffs. (They named the same game either "The Community Game" or "The Wall Street Game" and discovered that the name of the game completely trumped the premeasured personality of the players in predicting X or Y moves.)[14] As labels and tags are increasingly common in both political economic reporting and discussions, in all forms of media communications, this is a critical finding.

Second, when we run this exercise, the individual players are told to maximize their own payoff. Making this individual gain frame salient increases the tendency for players to "defect" by playing X when others play Y, thus gaining at the others' expense. It is worth noting, though, that even when we give no such instruction and instead let players decide what the word *you* means in the title (singular or plural) and what *win* means (maximize points, distribute points evenly, etc.), they rarely create $100 in value—and a sizable number of exercises end up with all four players having *lost* money by the end! Yet in business environments an individual-gain frame usually dominates, regardless of (in some cases) rhetoric to the contrary.

Third, we permit only brief communication before rounds 5, 8 and 10. This makes it much harder for players to create explicit agreements among themselves and to think of ways to "punish" those who do not comply with the agreements.

This exercise illustrates two critical dilemmas faced by organizations and their employees. The first dilemma, sometimes called the *negotiator's dilemma*, focuses on cooperation and vulnerability: how can we promote cooperative behavior that will help everyone do well, while avoiding exploitation if we choose to be cooperative but others do not? The second dilemma involves time frames and reputations: how can we highlight that this is not a one-shot deal? How can we suggest or show that distrust has demonstrably harmful effects on future payouts?

We describe these dilemmas in the context of an abstract exercise, but we believe they lie at the heart of the dissociation we often observe between organizational intentions and daily behaviors. Negotiators, leaders, and decision makers like to talk about teamwork and collaboration, but their actions and decisions often undermine it. They talk about the importance of creating value for customers, suppliers, employees, and their communities; yet when push comes to shove they put a priority on claiming value that undermines reputations, relationships, and opportunities in the long term, and that increases risk and costs as well. Take for example:

- Sales managers who push products that customers don't really need, pocketing a commission but leaving support staff to cope with the resulting unhappiness

- Team leaders who push their people too hard, or without sufficient praise or guidance, toward meeting a goal (deadline, cost reduction) but lose personnel who decide to leave

- Financial leaders who cut staff or technology or R&D to save money in the short term, creating long-term problems and losses

- Procurement leaders or consultants who focus too much on cutting quarterly spending without adequately accounting for the increased risk generated or the loss in innovation by the supplier

- Executives who reward themselves and others for meeting quarterly earnings estimates or delivering on other promises, no matter how such results are achieved

It should be clear that each of these examples fails to satisfy our seven criteria for evaluating negotiation success listed in chapter 3.

Step 8 stressed the importance of measuring and rewarding behavior consistent with business strategy, while adhering to our criteria for negotiation success. The tenth step requires that leaders (1) set forth explicit values; (2) make it clear that everyone, including leaders, is accountable for embracing those values; (3) take steps to define precisely what the values mean in terms of business processes (like negotiation); and (4) measure results and reinforce desired behaviors accordingly. As we've seen, negotiation is one critical and recurring arena in which values are either upheld, betrayed, or blurred/rationalized away.

The Power and Limits of Values

A Web search for the phrase *corporate values* turns up pages from companies like Boeing, IBM, Microsoft, and Whole Foods sharing with the world the values that they embrace. You'll also see books and articles that describe the critical function that values play. Milton Rokeach conducted a seminal line of research nearly forty years ago, distinguishing between *terminal values* (ends we wish to achieve) and *instrumental values* (ways we wish to behave in achieving those ends).[15] Many organizations have adopted lists of values (sometimes startlingly long!) that employees and leaders are expected to uphold. Most often these are a mix of terminal (e.g., deliver high value to customers), and instrumental (behave in an ethical manner at all times).

Critics may well point out that companies have often developed value statements reactively or defensively, following some scandal or misbehavior, to reassure the public—and their employees—that their ends *and* means are noble. Critics will further assert that such lists or pronouncements are in most cases unlikely to produce meaningful change in key daily behaviors. Attitudes, after all, have generally been found by social psychologists to be weak predictors of relevant behaviors across a wide variety of contexts.

There is merit in this critique. Too often, companies spend time and effort on "values statements" that have little to do with the kinds of pressure and dilemmas faced by their leaders and employees. Moreover, setting up organization values can lead to cynicism when actions by leaders are construed as hypocritical. Yet under some conditions, where values truly generate organizational norms ("the way we do things") an argument can be made that they do meaningfully influence behavior and decisions at critical moments.

There are persistent reports from leaders and consultants that values matter, and we take those seriously. A 2005 study undertaken by Booz Allen and the Aspen Institute surveyed a large sample of corporate leaders to identify how companies define corporate values, as well as best practice for managing them. Among the core findings, based on responses from more than 360 executives: *ethical behavior* was the most commonly cited corporate value (cited by 90 percent of the respondents) followed closely by *commitment to customers*. Third and fourth were *commitment to employees* and *teamwork and trust*. How do companies align values with their strategy? The survey suggests that leaders see values affecting relationships and reputation, but not affecting revenue growth, and other key operational metrics. The management practice cited as most effective in reinforcing corporate values was *explicit CEO support*.[16]

Bill George, the former CEO of Medtronic, has emphasized the importance of authenticity in his writing about leadership, arguing that effective leaders (who build trust to gain followers) must feel authentic in their roles. In the course of conversations with a number of leaders we've heard firsthand about their beliefs about values and their willingness to communicate the importance of values every day (see "Corning Lives Its Corporate Values").

Evidence That Values Matter

Yet more is needed than belief. Where is the evidence that values and institutional culture matter? We find evidence in disparate quarters.

In one innovative analysis, investment manager Jay Bragdon researched companies that convey a deep respect for life in the ways they treat employees, strategic partners, communities, and the environment.[17] A common attribute of these firms was their practice of placing a higher value on living assets (people and natural ecosystems) than on nonliving capital assets—an approach he called *living asset stewardship* (LAS).

To measure the effectiveness of such companies Bragdon created a learning lab of sixty global corporations—called the *global living asset management performance* (LAMP) index—that were stewardship exemplars in diverse industry/sectors. Tests run by

Corning Lives Its Corporate Values

One company that has lived by values for 150 years is Corning. In 2000–2001 the company (along with many technology companies in the telecommunications sector) saw its stock price collapse from $20 to $1. Called out of retirement to again take the reins as CEO, Corning's chairman, James Houghton, was faced with difficult decisions as he sat down to address the company's senior leaders. During its 150 years the company had become known for a spirit of innovation, teamwork, and social responsibility. Still, Houghton faced difficult choices. His leaders needed guidance on whether and how the company would survive.

Houghton decided to talk about his own and the company's beliefs and values. He was on record as saying that "Today, more than ever, there's a public recognition that values and honest business behavior really do matter . . . and that a good reputation is an asset precious beyond belief."[a]

Houghton convened a meeting with the corporate management group (the company's two hundred top leaders worldwide). He reminded them of the seven values that Corning had officially adopted a

the investment consultancy Northfield Information Services affirmed that the average stock market results of these sixty firms led the S&P 500 and the MSCI World indices every year from 1996 through 2007. Returns weighted by market capitalization were equally impressive, a finding Northfield describes as both economically and statistically significant. Also noteworthy, the average and median ages of companies in the LAMP index exceeded a century—more than double the lifespan of the average exchange-listed corporation. Bragdon attributes these extraordinary findings to the trust and loyalty these companies built with employees, customers, and other stakeholders. This set of find-

decade earlier: quality, integrity, performance, leadership, innovation, independence, and the individual. After talking about the importance of living by these values—particularly in difficult times—Houghton outlined the conditions for success at Corning. These included not only commitment to a common set of values, but also profitability as a necessary, but not sufficient, condition for success. He said, paraphrasing leadership theorist Charles Handy, "The purpose of a business is not to make a profit. It is to make a profit so that the business can do something more or better. That something becomes the real justification for the business."[b] In addition, Houghton emphasized that the company needed to focus on meeting the needs of *major stakeholders*—its long-term shareholders and employees.

Above all, Houghton has emphasized a commitment to creating long-term value. As he told us, "In this high-tech world we live in, anybody who does not take a long view is making a serious mistake."

Since those dark days in 2002 Corning has bounced back, besting many of its competitors and, at the date of writing, boasting a stock price of $24.

a. In "Our Values," Corning's official statement of values. b. Charles Handy, *The Age of Paradox* (Boston, Mass: Harvard Business Press, 2005).

ings suggests that corporate values, both terminal and instrumental, may indeed be an important factor in bottom line success.

A second line of indirect evidence that values and standards matter involves experiments conducted by Jared Curhan and his colleagues. Working with complex modeling techniques and measuring how negotiators do over time in repeated negotiations with counterparts in "open markets," these researchers have shown that negotiators are most likely to want to negotiate again with a partner when they feel good about the outcome, the process, the relationship, and *themselves*. In these studies, what economists call *subjective value*—how parties feel after an experience—

turned out to be a better predictor of future behavior than any other indicator.[18] So, while we have proposed seven success criteria in evaluating negotiations from the standpoint of the organization, adhering to one's own internal standards or personal values may also matter.

Under what conditions are values more likely to have an impact? This seems to us the critical question. In our view, values are most likely to influence behavior meaningfully when they are:

1. Created in advance of crises, rather than during them

2. Limited in number

3. Publicly and passionately endorsed by leadership

4. Clearly understood by employees, using exemplar stories that involve real dilemmas, particularly dilemmas that involve competing values

5. Coupled with a culture of candor, in which employees feel permission to question actions or decisions where they feel values have been violated

6. Aligned with performance incentives

Simply talking about values and going through extensive processes to create pieces of paper that have values written on them, is not likely to affect behaviors. In their 2006 case study of a marketing firm, Cha and Edmonson observed that it is easy for leaders to lose sight of the fact that their employees may construe values more expansively than they do, or to infer motives for decisions or actions that are not informed by information and perspective that the leader brought to the problem.[19]

Sadly, there are many examples of companies (Enron, Tyco, Adelphia, etc.) that have failed to create a culture of candor, and which have seen their reputations plummet after gross violations of values were uncovered. There has been less attention to aligning values with key performance incentives. The Booz Allen study, for example, found no clear "best practices" around measuring and rewarding adherence to values.[20]

We see alignment with incentives as a critical issue for leaders to address. As we discussed in chapter 3, when organizations ask us to help them improve their negotiation outcomes, we begin with an assessment, and ask for stories about difficult negotiations. Notwithstanding each organization's belief that it alone has certain kinds of dysfunctions around negotiation, we observe the same problems repeatedly across contexts, some of these involve missing information or lack of clarity around mandate. But in many instances—particularly in internal negotiations—leaders and managers find themselves operating with competing values and goals.

For example, since 2001, a common mandate for leaders in large organizations has sounded something like this: "Find a way to cut costs; increase productivity; don't incur unreasonable risks." This (complex!) imperative becomes even more challenging when it must also accommodate company values like "teamwork" and "customers come first." We've argued that part of preparing for negotiations and joint decision making is to clarify one's mandate. Negotiators can be more effective when they understand how results will be evaluated. We offered seven criteria for negotiation success, but it should be clear that values and standards, both personal and organizational, also matter. Discussing how to weigh the criteria and how to align corporate values and success criteria is likely to help negotiators and their constituents to identify trade-offs together, paving the way for more flexibility at the table.

Two-Way Accountability and Good Governance

Linking values and negotiation success criteria to incentives is a challenge. Companies must decide how to measure success. HP's Indirect Procurement team developed a scorecard that included financial savings/gains, process cost reduction (time to agreement and hours spent), and risk reduction (including risk from bad relationships or reputations). This scorecard was held up as a standard for all of their most important negotiations, evaluating billions of dollars in deals through a lens that is compatible with both a mutual gains approach and their existing business processes and tools. Just as important, they created a business process that required much more preparation, using the mutual gains approach as a guide and involving deal signatories and stakeholders to a much greater degree up front. The effect, as we've described, was beneficial.

Such efforts are critical. But so too is the willingness of leadership to be accountable to the values and success criteria that they expect others to follow. Educating group leaders in advance of each key deal about the group's BATNA, interests, aspirations, potential value creating moves, and so forth, makes the negotiators more accountable during preparation, but the leaders more accountable at the end. It is also likely to improve the quality of the deal, and the ease with which it is evaluated and approved.

When leaders are seen as making decisions that generate executive bonuses for themselves while harming employees, their communities, and/or customers, it is hard to expect negotiators on their behalf to take a mutual gains approach seriously. When negotiators are told by their leaders to use the company's leverage to force key suppliers to accept price reductions, to force uniquely capable distributors or sales partners to take on more risk, or to force a research partner to give up intellectual property, they are ensuring that their counterparts at the negotiation table will listen with cynicism at future negotiations about the desire to create value together. The dissociation we see between negotiations and corporate rhetoric can lead to employee turnover and supplier retribution in the form of hidden price increases, delays in delivery, poor customer service, and reticence or recrimination (rather than transparency and joint brainstorming) when risks or challenges are looming.

The Problem of Short-Termism

Are executives who say one thing but do another hypocrites by nature? Are they manipulative cynics who believe that saying nice things while playing hardball will win influence and market share? Notwithstanding plummeting public trust in corporations over the last decade, we don't leap to this conclusion. It is true that generous executive compensation—particularly in cases where large cash payouts have followed poor company performance—has exacted a toll on employee patience and public reputation. In the absence of data supporting the effectiveness of such compensation strategies, we agree with calls for reform of executive compensation, to more closely link pay to long-term performance across measures that go beyond revenue and profit to include adherence to the values that the company endorses for itself. But we believe that the culprit is primarily the way that financial performance is reported, evaluated, and rewarded. Although there are certainly bad apples out there, our experience is that most leaders are consciously conflicted about the dilemmas they face, but with the pressures that are present, they ultimately "do what is required" over and over again, perhaps staving off losses in the short term, but destroying value over the long term.

In recent years, leaders have all too often fallen into a pattern of managing to quarterly earnings estimates, jettisoning their cherished beliefs and rhetoric and regressing to destructive behaviors when short-term revenues or margins are threatened. This *short-termism* is a problem that academic institutions as well as business leaders are beginning to address.

From 2005 through 2006, the Business Roundtable Institute for Corporate Ethics, along with the Centre for Financial Markets Integrity, sponsored a "Symposium Series on Short-Termism." The series invited a frank dialogue among corporate business leaders, analysts, asset and hedge fund managers, and individual and institutional investors to talk about how corporate and investment decisions driven by short-term earnings goals often produces harmful consequences. The consensus that emerged was that the obsession with short-term results had the unintended consequence of destroying long-term value, decreasing market efficiency, reducing investment returns, and impeding efforts to strengthen corporate governance.

The consensus of these real-world pundits jibed with research findings. In one survey of more than four hundred financial executives, 80 percent said that they would reduce spending on R&D, advertising, maintenance, and hiring to meet short-term earnings targets, and more than 50 percent said they would delay new projects, even if it meant sacrificing value creation.[21] In recent years companies such as Intel, McDonald's, Motorola, and Pfizer have decided to scale back earnings guidance.

The participants at the symposium issued specific prescriptions for leaders, investors and analysts, urging them to:

1. End the practice of quarterly earnings guidance, or else move to a guidance format that focuses on providing higher-quality information focusing on long-term goals and strategy

2. Align corporate compensation to reward attainment of long-term strategic and value-creation goals, rather than annual profits or share price

3. Align asset managers' compensation with long-term performance and long-term client interests, and encourage disclosure of their incentives and fee structures

4. Promote a focus on long-term value by institutional investors, particularly when evaluating their asset managers[22]

The sponsors of the symposium also proposed a template for providing quarterly earnings that would allow apples-to-apples comparisons across companies by the investor community.

Such prescriptions echo similar calls from other quarters. For example, a 2006 McKinsey report entitled "The misguided practice of earnings guidance" found no evidence that quarterly earnings guidance had deleterious rather than beneficial effects: "Our analysis . . . found no evidence that [earnings guidance] affects valuation multiples, improves shareholder returns, or reduces share price volatility. The only significant effect we observe is an increase in trading volumes when companies start issuing guidance . . . [P]roviding quarterly guidance has real costs, chief among them the time senior management must spend preparing the reports and an excessive focus on short-term results."[23]

Let us be clear. We believe it is possible to improve negotiations in the ways we've described by adopting a mutual gains approach, even in companies that fall prey to behaviors and decisions driven by short-term earnings. That is, one can teach and support leaders and managers who want to create more valuable agreements, more efficiently, in ways that preserve trust and reputation. One can provide organizational learning opportunities, hold up examples of success, provide coaching and other resources, and work to overcome persistent barriers. But doing this is much more difficult in companies where leadership periodically takes a "make the numbers at any cost" stance. When organizational leaders behave in ways that contradict the values and success criteria they have enumerated, champions will find themselves swimming against a credibility undertow.

The Negotiating Organization: A Strategic Advantage

Organizational values, and the key leadership decisions and behaviors that affirm or contradict them, together comprise what we might call an *organizational culture*: a set of norms and beliefs about how things are done and what really counts. When one is trying to build a world-class negotiating organization, organizational culture is like soil. Planting the seeds of a new approach in poor soil will reduce the likelihood of real transformation. Planting seeds in a receptive and rich soil will accelerate growth. Rich soil is neither necessary nor sufficient—but it sure helps!

The tenth step works best when it comes *before* the other nine. It can help in moving through all of the other steps and stages. At the same time, as we have suggested, leaders may need to be confronted with the trade-offs that they are making (sometimes without fully realizing it). It would be a mistake to set up a rigid test, prior to trying to improve negotiations, requiring leaders to have demonstrated a focus on long-term value. In some cases, the effort to build a world-class negotiation practice will help leaders and managers to engage in critical dialogue about the company's current and future state. As we suggested at the outset of this book, negotiation represents an opportunity to improve not only the performance of negotiators, but the value proposition(s) of the organization.

While we have emphasized the critical role that sponsors and champions can play in creating a world-class negotiating organization, we have also seen that change can start anywhere from within an organization. Too often managers and staff wait for change to be mandated rather than pushing back on the organization and suggesting ways of improving processes and aligning incentives. Change can come from every level. Therefore, in chapter 6 we end "with the start in mind," describing the concrete and practical things individuals might do to steer their organization toward improvement.

$$\left[\ 6\ \right]$$

CONCLUSION: ENDING WITH THE START IN MIND

W E HAVE ARGUED that the time has come to stop paying for endless negotiation skills training and to help organizations implement the practices required to negotiate more effectively. We have provided a model for how to do this, while acknowledging that change in most organizations is often opportunistic and nonlinear. Let's look at some of the specific ways in which individual negotiators inside a company, organizational leaders, and HR professionals can—on their own—initiate efforts to build "winning" companies.

HOW INDIVIDUAL NEGOTIATORS CAN INITIATE CHANGE

We regularly hear from individual negotiators who see no way that they can, on their own, induce their company to make the changes required to support improved negotiation efforts. They assume that because they are not at the top of organization chart, they don't have the clout to make anything happen. But here are eight ways in which individual negotiators have been able to shape their company's approach to negotiation. ("An Individual Manager Can Make a Difference" provides an example of many of these practices in action.)

An Individual Manager Can Make a Difference

Jane is a sales manager of a well-known software company that recently branched out into the health-care field. She was responsible for selling the company's latest management software designed to help large hospitals handle increasingly complex client files in real time. At the urging of her CEO, who worried that the company was on track to miss the optimistic sales targets he had to accept to satisfy new investors, Jane attended an intensive two week senior executive training program in negotiation offered by one of America's most highly respected business schools. The program cut deeply into the time she would have had available to pursue potential clients, but it seemed worth it. She came back energized, focused, and armed with a half a dozen new ideas for improving her negotiation performance. She was confident these would help her close important deals relatively quickly. She intended to deploy these new techniques, particularly the tools for generating value-creating "packages" and the communication strategies for deflecting the hardball tactics so typical in her industry.

The first thing she discovered was that her company did not routinely collect information about potential clients' interests and perceived alternatives. Without this information, it would be hard to prepare in the way the trainers indicated was important. Jane sought additional funding to hire an outside consultant to collect this information, but was turned down. Rather than abandoning the new approach, she prepared a memo outlining how and why the information

1. They can *point out how improved negotiation practices
   will make it easier to meet organizational goals and
   objectives*, both in the short term and the long term. Too
   many people interested in negotiation improvements talk
   too much about *process* and not enough about how such
   improvements can lead to better *outcomes*. The best way to

---

she needed could be used to generate more lucrative deals. She
grounded her appeal for funds in the value-creating language she
had learned at the executive training program—spelling out the benefit to the company of being able to walk into each negotiation with
multiple, preapproved packages responsive to the most pressing concerns facing each potential client. She also offered to document the
ways in which the information she was requesting actually contributed
to the success of upcoming negotiations and, if it turned out to be
helpful (as she imagined it would), to prepare a short internal training program for other sales managers so they could achieve the
same results. She estimated the value added of the new information
by calculating the cost of acquiring it and speculating on the additional
amount she might be able to charge potential clients for specialized
versions of the company's new software product and the services to
support them.

Jane's willingness to document her efforts (regardless of how they
turned out) and to speculate on the potential value added of the
higher-level of negotiation preparation she was trying to implement, as
well as her willingness to take what she learned and help the organization use it to ongoing advantage, were enough to get her budget request approved. She took a risk, of course. There was no guarantee
that the new approach to negotiation preparation she proposed, and
the internal negotiations required to turn the results of her analysis into
approved offers she could put on the table, would generate the value
added she had predicted. On the other hand, if Jane were successful,
the company's attitude toward investing in negotiation preparation
might change in a very significant way.

capture the interest of top-level managers is to show them
the connections between improved negotiation practice
and specific results—like short-term financial gains,
improved odds of renewing key contracts, or an increase
in market share. And such claims are not unreasonable.
Within six to eight weeks of attending tailored training
sessions—coupled with modifications in longtime
operating practices—negotiators at all levels can show
measurable gains that have fallen to the bottom line.

2. They can *hold a mirror up to the inconsistencies between
   what is taught in company-sponsored negotiation training
   sessions and the operating practices that undercut the
   efforts of trainees to use what they have learned.* Most
   efforts to improve negotiating practices will rock the boat.
   You can't just add a new approach to negotiation to the
   usual ways of doing business. You have to cease doing
   certain things the old way. By spotlighting the inconsistencies between negotiation principles and practices presented
   in tailored training programs and the traditional company
   approach to preparing, dealing with negotiating partners,
   working internally to review draft agreements, and finalizing agreements, a lone advocate for negotiation improvement can, in fact, set the wheels of reform in motion.

3. They can *model best practices* within the existing framework of organizational norms and operating procedures.
   For example, they can use the checklists provided in
   appendix C and share them with colleagues and super-
   visors. Moreover, if advocates of negotiation reform are
   not prepared to act in the way they are urging others to
   act, they are not likely to be taken seriously. So any
   individual in any organization can use the preparation,
   value-creation, and implementation checklists we have
   presented. And they can focus their conversations with
   others on the analyses they produce. Colleagues will take

notice. While it may be difficult to work around certain operating practices that make it hard to use a mutual gains approach, negotiators who use the checklists will be better prepared to create value—regardless of the approach to negotiation that others are using. For instance, until word comes from the top that everyone across the organization should do what they can to help others clarify the company's BATNA in each upcoming negotiation, the preparation worksheet will encourage and assist people who try to do this on their own. It doesn't matter where in the corporate hierarchy negotiators are; they can make their own effort to specify what the company's BATNA might be and ask others to react. A concerted effort to model best practice will encourage others to do the same.

4. They can *serve as champions for the use of a consistent theory of negotiation* (such as the mutual gains approach). This will encourage the adoption of a common language for describing what is and isn't happening in particular negotiations. Using terms that others haven't heard might feel a bit awkward at first, but a concerted effort to define key terms every time they are used will eventually win converts.

5. They can *use required training sessions to provide feedback about the ways in which current operating procedures or attitudes stand in the way of using what they are being taught.* We often set aside time at the end of each tailored negotiation training session for participants to speculate on the problems they are likely to face when they try to use what they have just learned. It doesn't take long for a list of the most worrisome potential obstacles to emerge. In addition, we encourage trainees to think out loud about the kinds of support (like ongoing coaching) they might find helpful. We then ask those present whom they think should get a copy of these lists. Sometimes one

person in the group is willing to take our draft summary to the right person in the organization. Sometimes they ask us to do it. In either case, the lists are presented as a by-product of the training the company has purchased. When someone inside takes the lists forward, they don't necessarily have to "own" them personally.

6. They can *work with others to push for negotiation audits* at various scales. A negotiation audit is a relatively inexpensive way to document how well an organization is handling negotiation crucial to its survival. There are outside experts who know how to produce such analyses. Someone may not be high enough up in an organization to advocate the full set of negotiation improvements described in this book, but might be able to commission a negotiation audit for the section or unit he or she manages. The results are likely to be instructive for others and generate the moment required to implement organization-wide negotiation audits.

7. They can offer to *serve as a sounding board (if not a coach) for others who are frustrated because what is being taught in negotiation training sessions is hard to implement.* It is easy to get frustrated when the same organization that sent staff to a high-powered training session designed to improve their negotiation skills refuses to realize that these people can't use what they were taught unless changes are made in operating procedures and reward systems. Usually, at the first sign of resistance, newly trained negotiators bail. That is, they revert to whatever way they negotiated before they took the training. A bit of encouragement at such a moment can be crucial. It is very difficult to be the only person trying to do things in a new way—and there is a chance of being treated as a pariah. But two people—or a small coalition—trying to do things in a new way is tantamount to a reform move-

ment! If you can provide encouragement and support to just one other person until organizational practices are adjusted, you can help promote negotiation reform.

8. They can *document their own negotiation efforts and volunteer the results for case studies of current organizational practice*. Organizational learning requires systematic reflection. Sometimes, though, a close study of what happened in a particular negotiation can lead to the conclusion that someone did a poor job. Too few people are willing to be the focus of a case study of a failed negotiation effort. Studies of failed negotiation can be even more instructive than great success stories. The only way organizational learning will occur is if key personnel cooperate by documenting their negotiation practices even if that makes them look bad. Why would they do this? If senior management rewards such openness, others will agree to participate. Real stories can be fictionalized to protect reputations. As long as everyone knows the story is a faithful account of what happened, but the names are disguised to protect reputations, the learning effect will be substantial. Those who want to promote negotiation reform in their organization can volunteer to be the focus of a case study. They may become heroes if the story showing what they did wrong helps others avoid similar mistakes and helps the company to make important organizational improvements.

HOW ORGANIZATIONAL LEADERS CAN CHAMPION CHANGE

There are many models and theories of leadership. One that we find particularly appealing is called *facilitative leadership*. A facilitative leader doesn't demand improved performance; he or she makes it easier for others to achieve their goals. Here are ten ways in which facilitative leaders can champion changes that lead to enhanced organizational negotiating capabilities.

1. The first and most important step that leaders can take is to assert that *negotiation is a core organizational competence, and not just an individual skill.* This is not hard to do, but the commitment will be meaningful only if the leader devotes sufficient resources to implement the idea. And the commitment will produce results only if the leadership is prepared to stick with the idea for the several years it takes to move through the ten steps outlined in the course of this book.

2. Leaders can have a dramatic effect by *adopting a consistent model or language for gauging the effectiveness of a company's negotiation efforts.* This means not only urging everyone to take a tailored training program that introduces them to useful negotiation nomenclature, but also using that same language (and the fundamental model or theory it implies) whenever they talk about negotiation. This also means that corporate leaders can't just send everyone who works for them to the training; they have to go themselves.

3. Leaders can *insist that all employees, particularly top managers, use the kinds of checklists provided in appendix C.* They can make it clear that they, too, are using these checklists. This demonstrates a commitment to a common negotiation language and theory. It also makes it easier to harmonize the disparate negotiation efforts of different departments or divisions.

4. A leader can *insist that a systematic negotiation audit be undertaken* by a qualified external negotiation expert. We have described how that would work. The responsibility of the leader is to prompt such an effort and to make sure

it is handled by someone in the organization who can make good use of the findings.

5. A leader can *commit to make the results of a negotiation audit visible,* even if they reflect on the leadership's negotiating performance in a less than flattering way. This will increase the legitimacy of the audit and the recommendations that emerge from it.

6. A leader can *invest the resources necessary to support the development of tailored negotiation training as well as experiments* aimed at strengthening the organization's negotiating capabilities (in light of the audit results). The leader must be savvy enough, of course, to select experiments that will provide leverage for organization-wide change.

7. A leader can *encourage participants in training programs to provide feedback*, both at the training session and afterward, regarding apparent inconsistencies between what was taught and the usual practices of the organization. If criticism is viewed as a sign of disloyalty, however, continuous improvement will not be possible. It is up to the leader to make clear that constructive feedback is welcomed (and perhaps even rewarded).

8. A leader can *benchmark, reward, and publicize efforts to improve individual, group and organizational negotiation performance.* This might include rewarding risk takers willing to experiment with new negotiation techniques and methods. It might take the form of bonuses for negotiators who can document the value they have added by applying new negotiation techniques or strategies being promoted by the company.

9. A leader can *support the implementation of an organization-wide center of excellence* through which negotiation coaching and other forms of assistance can be delivered.

Coaching can be provided through online communities in ways that don't require anyone to acknowledge publicly that they are not fully confident in their negotiation skills.

10. Finally, a leader must *acknowledge that efforts to enhance organizational negotiating capabilities require constant and ongoing attention.* Enhancing organizational negotiating capability requires a multiyear effort. While it is perfectly reasonable to specify short-term targets or success, it is not possible to build long-term negotiating capacity without several years of concerted effort.

Case: The Role of Leadership Is Crucial

Terry is the CFO of a midsized engineering firm that manages bridge and highway projects and the building of sewage treatment facilities and oversees the construction of public buildings. Most of the construction management work the firm does requires it to bid on contracts from a range of federal and state agencies. Terry has recently concluded that it will be harder than ever over the next year or two to land major projects, given the current economic climate. He also knows that the company will be squeezed in every future contract negotiation by government agencies trying desperately to reduce costs. Terry's company will have to demand more for less from its subcontractors and construction partners or it won't survive. Not a pleasant thought.

Terry believes that improved negotiations across the board—with clients, suppliers, subcontactors, and strategic partners and even internally among departments—hold the key to profitability in tough times. At the same time, repeat business will continue to be essential to his company's growth. It has worked hard for decades to maintain good working relationships with every client. So, the puzzle for

Terry is how to negotiate more profitable agreements while at the same time maintaining customer satisfaction and good working relationships.

Terry doesn't often take the lead in devising corporate strategy. His company's founder and CEO, along with its general counsel and CFO, do the strategic thinking. It is Terry's job to make sure the money is there, the bills get paid, and everybody gets to take home a good salary. Now, though, he is convinced that a modest improvement in each contract negotiation holds the key to the organization's long-term financial survival. He's not sure, though, how to pursue this objective. Based on what he has heard and read, as well as his own propensity to set numerical goals, Terry wants to set specific targets for negotiation improvement.

If each of the firm's three largest projects—all of which are scheduled to extend at least another eighteen months—produced an additional 3 percent in net revenue over the next twelve months, the company would have no problem exceeding its financial targets for the first half of the next fiscal year. So Terry has been trying to figure out whether it might be possible to renegotiate certain aspects of these three contracts. Because his company secured all three projects through competitive bids, it will be tough to get the agencies involved to contemplate changing the current contract terms.

Terry has an idea, though. What if, given all the pressures on the government agencies involved to reduce costs, Terry's project teams could find ways of saving money by working smarter? Now that they are in the middle of these projects, they have a much better idea of what it will take to finish each one than they did when they submitted their initial bids. Perhaps some kind of performance bonus or profit-sharing kicker could be suggested to each of the agencies involved. What would it take to make this happen? General counsel will have to figure out the legal arguments. Each project leader will have to come up with some way to save money, reduce the time it takes to get the job done, or modify some aspect of the project to save the client money in the long run.

Terry has decided that he's going to call together the key players involved in each project, along with the management team, to explore ideas for amending each contract. He knows that most of these people have no real understanding of how contract negotiations work—they usually leave it to him to piece together the bids and to negotiate the contract details, and then legal counsel reviews them. But in this instance, he doesn't know what specific changes in the timing, organization, or other aspects of each work plan might yield benefits for both sides. He needs everyone's help if 3 percent is to be added to the net profitability of each project.

It occurs to Terry that it might be useful to spend at least part of a day with the thirty or so people he intends to invite, getting them up to speed on the concept of value creation in negotiation. He won't call it training because they are much too busy to take time off for training. But he needs some way to get them to embrace a value-creating mind-set and open up to the possibility that the detailed project management plans they worked so hard to put in place could be adjusted. He knows they'll dislike the idea. Going over past practices in his mind, Terry realizes that his company has almost no negotiating capability other than what he brings to the table. Now, he needs to get everyone to see that they all have a role to play in renegotiating these contracts. They all need to understand how and why this might be possible. They also need a common language to facilitate consideration of possible value creating strategies. They'll need ongoing coaching and support. Most of all, individuals will have to realize that almost everything they do is connected in some way to what can be accomplished through renegotiation of these contracts. Terry can set the target, get them to see that they have a role to play, arrange to give them training and ongoing coaching, and make sure the company's normal operating procedures don't get in the way of the search for more profitable ways of meeting their contractual obligations. The rest will be up to them.

HOW HR LEADERS CAN SUPPORT CHANGE AND LEARNING

Human resource professionals have a central role to play in building a world-class negotiating organization. But this requires that many HR departments expand their mandate to go beyond individual skill building and accept responsibility for organizational learning. Here are six ways in which HR managers can support the changes and learning required to build organizational negotiating competence:

1. HR leaders can fight hard to *add responsibility for improving organizational negotiation performance to their mandate.*

2. HR leaders *can move away from prepackaged negotiation training to tailored negotiation training* following a systematic negotiation audit undertaken by a qualified outside professional.

3. HR leaders can *commit to quantitative evaluations of the impacts of the negotiation training they implement.* We have described in some detail how this might be done.

4. HR leaders can partner with internal customers to *inventory the obstacles to using what is taught in tailored negotiation training programs and assist in experimental efforts to* overcome them. The audit results and interaction with trainees will pinpoint where the work needs to be done.

5. HR leaders can *add negotiation coaching to the list of things for which HR is prepared to take responsibility.*

This might involve building an on-line learning portal to deliver negotiation support and coaching to anyone in the organization who needs it. Such assistance can be provided anonymously.

6. Finally, and perhaps most important, HR leaders can *advocate for the inclusion of negotiation performance* as part of annual job performance reviews. This would mean working with each department or division to formulate ways of benchmaking relevant negotiation results in ways that make sense to everyone involved. And, such assessments should lead to bonuses or salary modifications.

HR Leaders Have a Special Role to Play

Mary is the HR director at a national financial services firm with more than twenty thousand employees in eight states. All new hires are required to take a one-week introductory training program, including a day-long unit covering the basics of negotiation. Anyone at or above the third level of the firm's five-level personnel hierarchy must take Level II negotiation training provided at three company locations five times a year. Mary has contracted with a well-known negotiation training firm to provide these Level II courses to more than three thousand people annually. Evaluations collected at the end of the each two-day Level II course show an average rating of 3.7 on a 1–5 scale (where 5 is excellent, 4 is very good, 3 is good, 2 is fair, and 1 is poor). The cost is approximately $400,000 a year or $200 per trainee (not counting the cost of travel).

Mary is being pressed by top management to demonstrate that there is a return on this annual investment. Focus group discussions with a number of trainees have convinced Mary that it will be difficult to justify continuing to spend this much money every year. Very few of the focus group participants have been able to point to specific negotiation results they attributed to the training, which for some had taken place several years earlier.

Mary decides to undertake a negotiation audit that could be used to design a tailored negotiation training program. From her standpoint, it makes more sense to offer a mid-level negotiation course (and perhaps several versions of it) to those who really *want* to take it. In addition, a tailored course could be designed to help managers at the top three organizational levels deal with the most important upcoming negotiations. Finally, Mary intends to launch a new negotiation learning portal on the company's intranet, to (1) allow those who take the intermediate course to stay in touch with each other and share stories describing their efforts to use what they have learned; (2) provide "anonymous" coaching online for staff who are nervous about asking for help directly; and (3) offer readings and templates (like the checklists in appendix C) to make it easier for company staff to use what they have been taught.

Mary is confident that through careful monitoring she'll be able to demonstrate specific instances in which negotiation results can be attributed to what people have learned in a tailored mid-level course or through the assistance they received via the learning portal. For two or three years, using the same annual budget she spends now for required mid-level training for two thousand people, Mary estimates she'll be able to serve five hundred top-level managers each year and more than five thousand employees at all levels through the learning portal. One possibility, although she'll have to raise it with the executive committee, is to devote some of the value added she can attribute to this new approach to training to performance bonuses for individuals as well as business units.

The first thing Mary is going to do is initiate a monthly negotiation eNewsletter. This will present brief stories highlighting especially interesting or instructive negotiations. With the help of a local business journalist and a selected negotiation-training firm, she expects to have monthly stories that will focus companywide attention on the importance of enhanced negotiation capabilities. She is even thinking of asking the CEO to sign a short (one-page) commentary in response to each case to demonstrate that concerns about improved negotiation have the attention of the top leadership.

CONCLUSION

If some consultants and trainers consider our suggestions radical, we won't object. But we hasten to add that the changes we have described do not require radical actions or commitments. They do require a clear picture of what the organization needs to do. They do require a commitment by the organization to look at current practices and be open to opportunities. They do require defining criteria for measuring success and aligning organizational structures, processes, and incentives with those criteria.

We don't think that these changes are beyond most organizations. Indeed, it is our sense most organizations have experienced the limitations of the training-only approach and are looking for something better. The tasks we have outlined produce the best results when leaders and staff seek to end with the beginning in mind. That is, each negotiation reform is a milestone along the way, pointing to how further improvement might be achieved. The flow of personnel in and out of every organization and the shifting business context in which every company works mean that negotiation strategies and tactics must be regularly evaluated and revised. A company that is built to win is one that is continuously improving. We hope the approach outlined in this book provides a clear way forward.

In the spirit of sustaining our own learning and sharing our experience, we invite you to join us in a further dialogue at: www.builttowinbook.com.

APPENDIX A

WHY TRAINING ALONE
OFTEN FAILS

Our efforts as consultants and trainers have focused on helping organizations and leaders negotiate more effectively. Because the stakes are high and tangible, negotiation improvements matter. When we began working with Hewlett-Packard in 2004, for instance, they were spending roughly $70 billion a year on goods and services, and many billions more on sales and distribution agreements. Enhancing negotiation effectiveness by 1 percent for a company like HP yields an additional $700 million a year in profit—the difference between a roaring success and a whopping failure.

Twenty-five years after *The Art and Science of Negotiation* and *Getting to Yes* hit bookstores, negotiation is widely recognized as a critical business skill, taught in MBA programs and law schools across the country.[1] Dispute resolution is an interdisciplinary topic of study at many colleges, and research on negotiation has been pursued from a number of starting points, including psychology, law, economics, game theory, public policy, and international relations. Negotiation is a core course in corporate learning curricula and executive education programs in many parts of the world. The American Society for Training and Development

(ASTD) in its *2008 State of the Industry Report*, estimated that organizations in the United States alone "spend $134.39 billion on employee learning and development annually, with nearly three quarters ($83.62 billion) spent on the internal learning function, and the remainder ($50.77 billion) spent on external services."[2] Assuming that negotiation might comprise 1 percent of all such training, then organizations in the United States spend at least a billion dollars annually on negotiation training.

This is an enormous investment. And yet, there are few indications that the way people are negotiating and the results they are achieving represent a measurable improvement. A recent review of published negotiation training outcome studies found only two instances in which return on investment had actually been tallied.[3] Having taught negotiation for many years, we have seen little evidence that trainees enter our classrooms today with better negotiation practices than trainees possessed two decades ago.

Worse, we have often found that organizations in which we have trained managers are not benefiting nearly as much as they could from the experience. We've read similar reports from colleagues and heard the same thing at conferences and symposia. Claims made by training companies on their Web sites evaporate when judged by basic experimental standards (like having an untrained control group). Still, in the absence of a clear alternative to training, organizations continue to invest heavily, exploring and embracing new forms of presentation (such as e-learning) but failing, in our view, to think strategically about ways to generate (or even measure) a higher return on investment (ROI).

If we know so much more about how to get to yes, why does it remain so difficult for organizations in a competitive world to reach satisfying agreements through efficient processes that protect and enhance relationships? In part, it is because while research over the last twenty-five years has generated a more robust general theory of negotiation, there has not been a corresponding increase in our knowledge of how people and organizations can consistently improve their negotiation results. Treating negotiation as an activity undertaken by two individuals across a table is no longer a realistic assumption when the negotiators are working on behalf of others, and within large networks of colleagues, bosses, and partners. In short, *off-the-shelf training is a weak intervention in a world where organizational systems, structures, and incentives are powerful.* Failing to strengthen the organization at the same time as we build individual negotiation capabilities will result in failure. The results of laboratory research demonstrate this, and in our work as trainers, coaches, and consultants, we too often hear real-world stories of lost opportunities, painful processes, and compromised relationships.[4] Why might this be? We see three possible reasons.

EXPLANATION #1:
POOR SKILLS TRAINING

The most common explanation for why training fails is that the training itself was poorly designed or delivered, and that skills were therefore not learned or improved. There is some merit to this critique; most negotiation training is off-the-shelf and involves fairly generic exercises, typically with a single buyer and a single seller. In some cases it is designed to elicit the highest scores on an evaluation sheet, so that the training company can claim measurable success. Consequently, there is an equal focus on educating and entertaining. A range of ideas and tactics are offered, but no sound process theory or model is provided. Even if materials are targeted to a particular industry, they are not tailored with sufficient skill or subtlety to address the problems that the audience actually faces.

The trouble with this approach to training is that negotiations and organizations are both much more complicated. In a world of globally networked, technologically complex, and strategically nimble competitors and systems, most negotiations are multilayered undertakings, rather than one-to-one transactions.

Although two parties might sit across a table, each typically represents the interests of different functions and teams who must live with the terms of any agreement and execute it successfully. Indeed, implementing commercial agreements can involve dozens of stakeholders whose interests and constraints need to be understood and considered in crafting a deal. This means that training only *some* of the parties who have to work together will create disconnections and knowledge gaps, both in terms of what needs to be done before, during, and after the face-to-face negotiation and in terms of what the organization needs to do to implement the deal. It is not enough for a single person to understand what is required to create and claim value while protecting relationships; *all* those who have a stake in the agreement and its implementation must understand what is at stake beyond their narrow interests, how success will be defined for all sides, and what procedures and considerations each negotiator is obliged to accept.

If you accept our critique, then you realize that organizations should insist that all training be tailored to its audience and based on a proven approach grounded in empirical research. Perhaps leaders and managers who are offered better, more relevant training, the argument goes, will go back to their organizations and behave differently. But will they?

Let's suppose that the leadership decides to give all key professionals in its organization negotiation training, and that the selected approach is rooted in a practical and proven theory (like the mutual gains approach), using carefully tailored simulations and cases. Suppose the firm they hire conducts confidential interviews with key executives in advance of the workshop to learn as much as they can about the most and least successful negotiations that have occurred in recent months. Suppose further that this information is used to diagnose the reasons for failure as well as opportunities for negotiation improvement—internal conflicts, missing data, unreasonable aspirations, poor insight into the other side's interests, time pressures, changing mandates, and so on. Suppose a program is designed to address these problems—rooted in a sound theory and delivered with skill.

But even well-designed training will fall short if it happens in a vacuum. We've seen enormous investments in training provided by excellent trainers from reputable organizations—including ours—lead to marginal or negligible ROI. Many of the executives and managers we've trained have told us in post-training evaluations that the workshop exceeded their expectations. We've followed up months and years later to see what has changed. Sadly, in too many cases—even those where the organization continued to spend millions on negotiation training annually—a common refrain is: "The workshop was great; we still talk about it . . . but have we changed? To be honest, not nearly enough."

EXPLANATION #2:
HUMAN FALLIBILITY

A second explanation is that change doesn't occur because training cannot overcome predictably irrational mistakes that negotiators (and the rest of us) usually make. After all, even highly capable negotiators are beset with self-serving biases and faulty beliefs that cause them to miss opportunities and arrive at needless impasses. Our several decades of empirical research supports the notion that we tend to see and judge people and situations in biased ways, with deleterious effects at the negotiating table.

Research by psychologists such as Dan Gilbert, Tim Wilson, Dan Ariely, Max Bazerman, Linda Babcock, Lee Ross, George Loewenstein, and Leigh Thompson sheds light on specific examples of how our perceptions and our reasoning tend to go awry.[5] Among their findings: Most people entering negotiations do not think with sufficient clarity about their own interests and alternatives or—a more egregious mistake—about the other side's perceived alternatives and interests. They fail to grasp what they themselves really want. They fail to surmise that the negotiation they face does not necessarily involve a fixed pie. They don't anticipate that there is more than one important issue on the table, or that their interests might complement their counterparts'. They routinely fail to capture all the value that was actually available. They readily fixate on numbers and place far too much weight on them—even numbers generated randomly (say, by a roulette wheel or by writing down the last digits of their social security numbers).

Negotiator judgment can be manipulated by framing decisions and choices strategically and by using carefully selected labels; such subtle manipulations turn out to dwarf personality variables. Negotiators regularly fail to imagine "predictable surprises" that will occur during the life of an agreement.

Aside from these cognitive failures, even experienced negotiators fall prey to *motivated reasoning*, that is, making egocentric and self-serving judgments about how well they did, what is fair, and what others will think. The more complex, ambiguous, and information-rich a situation is, the more likely the people involved are to be self-serving and faulty in their judgments about the nature of the problem and about other people. Negotiators are overly confident about their future performance, insight, and acumen while attributing unfavorable motives and traits to counterparts in situations where agreement looks like it will be difficult to achieve. They think the data they bring to the table is "objectively fair" and "most relevant"; but it is viewed with equal certainty as "biased" and "selective" by the other side. They tend to infer that moves by the other side reflect traits or beliefs of their counterpart ("he's just a competitive so-and-so"), and interpret such moves as conniving, exploitative, or unfair.[6] In short, people's negotiating behavior and decisions are very often suboptimal. And too often this means that value is not created and captured—even by experienced negotiators.

You may be reading this and thinking, "Well, that's not me." (So did the thousands of negotiators who were the subjects of these studies!) Or thinking, "Even if I did bring some biases, couldn't training help me overcome them?" There is research to be done in this area, but what little exists suggests that "debiasing" is an uphill battle. While it appears possible in some cases to help negotiators become more aware of certain traps, there are no documented cases we know of in which such effects have been carried back into real-world situations.[7] It is challenging enough to teach people to overcome their own cognitive limitations and biases, precisely because we are so unlikely to notice them in action, but it is even more challenging to expect people not to revert to these largely unconscious patterns once they return to the complex, uncertain, stressful, highly competitive, and rapidly changing situations in everyday life.

EXPLANATION #3:
IT'S THE CONTEXT, STUPID

The third explanation sounds like this: *Unless an organization is willing to define success and measure it, commit to clear process steps, and provide incentives and resources for reinforcing best practices, trainees will quickly fall back to current behavior.* Conventional training is like trying to explain to someone on a stationary bike how to ride in traffic on a real one. Talking about how to ride a bicycle, and offering a simulation of a ride, is a lot less effective than having the rider actually practice on a real bicycle in increasingly difficult and varied environments, and riding with others who are more experienced.

The idea is not new, and it too is rooted in a wealth of hard data. More than fifty years of research by social psychologists, across hundreds (perhaps thousands) of studies tell us that the structure of a situation and the forces within it tend to overwhelm individual attitudes and intentions.[8] Important elements of each negotiation context include the number of parties involved, the attractiveness of each party's alternative if there is no agreement, the form of communication possible among the parties, deadlines, and the presence or absence of audiences and/or constituents.

More specifically, structural and contextual factors influence negotiator perceptions, behavior, judgments, intentions, reasoning, strategy and outcomes. Power differentials matter; time constraints matter; alternatives matter; the degree and form of communication matters. This will come as no surprise to negotiators in the real world. A seller who is desperate for quick cash encounters a willing buyer and quickly agrees to a number that is close to the buyer's initial offer. Few would disagree that all other things being equal, the buyer would seem to wield more power.

And yet, research by Lee Ross and others suggests that our biases and situational variables interact in a powerful way: to some degree, situations are what we make of them; the way that we construe situations may be as important as the situations themselves.[9] A home seller *perceives* no other alternative to selling at a low price, but has not advertised the property effectively, and in his desperation never inquires about the buyer's needs and interests. A buyer is about to lose her current lease, loves the seller's place, and would gladly pay more than the seller's price. Both have imagined the wrong bargaining task and one or both will lose value they could have claimed. Or consider the converse: a seller finds himself in the catbird seat, but the buyer is in no hurry and has a great alternative to buying; the seller fumes when the offer is much lower than he expected, decides that the potential buyer is not serious, and breaks off further negotiations.

Precisely because our brains are prone to selective and biased processing, the structures and contexts we encounter are to some degree perceived, experienced, interpreted, and explained subjectively. And that turns out to be true not only with respect to our present experience; as Tim Wilson and Dan Gilbert have shown, our beliefs and explanations about the past and future can be influenced by factors about which we are unaware.[10]

Learning new behaviors requires knowing not just *what* to do (and what mistakes to try to avoid), but *how to* do it "back at the ranch." Negotiation involves a complex array of cognitive, behavioral, and affective processes, and single-event learning through lecture and role-playing is unlikely to unfreeze old habits, even when people have "a-ha" moments. As psychologists would put it, negotiation involves activating both *procedural* and *declarative* knowledge and memory systems. Procedural systems are activated when we ride a bike, swim, cook a dish for the tenth time, or play a musical instrument well. Declarative systems involve recall of facts like birthdays, phone numbers, names, and so forth. Anyone who has ever tried to give directions to a familiar location, but realizes that they don't know many of the relevant street names, has discovered that procedural memory is essential to our daily routines. Research suggests learning *what* is not the same as learning *how*, and that there are different neural systems involved.

How do people learn complex new behaviors, if not through lectures? In a striking study of negotiation and learning by Janice Nadler and her colleagues, trainees who watched an effective negotiation were more effective in a subsequent negotiation than those who had been told to listen to a lecture, or analyze a simulation with all of the "confidential" role information revealed.[11] When asked what they had done to create both joint and individual gains, however, they showed the least insight of any group. They had learned *how* without learning *what* they were doing.

As Albert Bandura noted thirty years ago, observational learning is a powerful learning mode, but it does not necessarily produce insight.[12] When individuals are sent to workshops to learn new skills, they leave their complex environment and enter one that is relatively free of context (e.g., context is defined by the instructor or role-play instructions). They listen to new ideas, are given a new process model grounded in sound research (if they are lucky), and get several chances to try out new behaviors and techniques. This may be good for learning the *what*, but it doesn't provide much opportunity to master the *how* under the kinds of conditions they will face in their work place. Even in on-site training, there is often little discussion of how new ideas and behaviors can be implemented and woven into everyday business processes.

Trainees rarely get to experiment with new skills or approaches in the high-stakes, time-pressured situations they find themselves in when they return to their complex and unchanged environments. While they might have learned that it is useful to prepare differently, or create new ground rules at the negotiating table, their colleagues are likely to resist doing things in a new way unless past results have been truly terrible. Even when newly trained team members come back with new ideas and models, it is hard for others to understand why the new approach might have merit or to trust that the additional work required is worth the effort. Moreover, some parties may be asked to play different roles, do more work, or give up authority that they had before. In such situations it is not hard to imagine why they might respond negatively.

WHICH EXPLANATION IS CORRECT?

They all are. That is, training is often badly designed or delivered. People are hard to change. And organizations and situational constraints are extremely powerful. But for too long analysis has focused narrowly on poor training and on individual learning failures as the locus of the problem. A lot of creative energy has been invested in developing new and different kinds of training for individuals, but very little has been focused on how to change and align organizational systems, processes, and incentives. Our focus is on ways of reducing the chances that individuals will fall prey to troublesome mental shortcuts, and on strategies for increasing the chances they get the support they need to create and claim value effectively at a wide range of negotiating tables.

Most organizations do not identify and support effective negotiation practice. But those that do will enjoy an enormous competitive advantage, particularly in a hypercompetitive world. Our central purposes in this book are to 1) lay out a prescriptive framework that is *realistic* in its assessment of the complex challenges facing a wide range of negotiators and *practical* for leaders seeking to address such complexity; and 2) to provide a theory of intervention that equips the organization to create the practices, measures, and incentives that will reinforce and support critical learning at critical moments.

NEGOTIATION STYLES AND BEHAVIORS

TABLE B-1

Negotiation styles and behaviors

Behaviors/styles	Tough	Soft	Mutual gains
Asking questions about others	Asks few questions	Asks few or indirect questions	Asks many questions to elicit interests, assumptions, priorities
Giving information	Provides little information	Provides all information	Provides information about interests but not bottom line
Trading/concessions	Doesn't want to trade	Willing to give up a lot in trades	Trades things less important in order to get things more important
Using fair standards	More interested in gain than fairness	Wants fairness but won't demand it	Insists on fairness and seeks reasonable standards for all groups
Maintaining relationships	Doesn't worry about relationship	Sacrifices achieving own interests for the relationship	Achieves own interests while maintaining a good relationship
Using power	Shows hostility, or no emotion; threatens, criticizes and bullies other side	Empathic; may share own feelings of vulnerability; shows anxiety or concern about provoking anger	Shows empathy, shares concerns, maintains emotional composure, hints at power without using it.

NEGOTIATION CHECKLISTS

Below are checklists designed to guide negotiators in the fundamentals of the mutual gains approach.

NEGOTIATIONS PREPARATION CHECKLIST

The following checklist presents a series of questions every negotiator should review with key stakeholders *prior to* meeting with a negotiating partner:

1. Who are we representing in this negotiation?

2. How will we prepare together?

3. What are our interests (in order of importance) in the upcoming negotiation?

4. What are the interests of the other side?

5. What is our BATNA (i.e., where would we stand if this deal fell through)?

6. How should we value our BATNA, in view of the costs and benefits, both short- and long-term?

7. How can we improve our BATNA?

8. What is their BATNA? How could we raise doubts about it, and/or make their BATNA less attractive?

9. What do we need to learn early in our conversation with the other side? From whom? How will we inquire?

10. What packages (bundles of options) can we put forward that meet their interests well and our interests very well?

11. What information do we need to collect to bolster arguments for options we favor? What criteria can we cite to persuade them that our proposals are fair?

12. What implementation problems are likely to arise if they accept our proposal and how might these be overcome?

VALUE-CREATION CHECKLIST

This checklist suggests analytical sources of value creation, reminds negotiators of behaviors that they ought to be practicing in order to encourage value creation, and suggests different forms that value might take:

Analytical Sources of Value Creation

1. What issues do we value differently?

2. What difference in resources or capabilities might we jointly exploit?

3. Does one of us have a higher tolerance for risk (on a particular issue or globally)?

4. Do we have different preferences or priorities around timing?

5. What other things might they value that we could provide at relatively low cost?

6. If we disagree about future scenarios or don't yet have all the data, what contingent agreements ("if ____, then ____") might we propose?

7. What issues are likely to produce positional bargaining, and how can we unbundle them into multiple issues (e.g., pricing becomes total price, timing, currency, etc)?

8. What other issues could we link to this deal? How might we broaden or narrow the deal to increase chances for mutual gain?

9. What options are we prepared to propose?

10. What are at least two packages (bundles of options) we can propose that will help us to avoid anchoring and issue-by-issue dynamics?

In-Session Behavior Checklist

1. How well are we listening? (Aim to listen 70 percent of the time in first meeting.)

2. Have we probed for interests by asking why? What are we learning?

3. Have we suspended criticism?

4. Have we explained why we need the things we need?

5. Are we spending enough time on "inventing without committing"?

6. Are we keeping our stakeholders' interests and constraints clearly in mind as we invent options?

Forms Value Can Take

Revenue	Profit	Cost/spend reduction
Future revenues	Reputation/brand	Future profits
Future savings	Quality improvement	Innovation
Risk mitigation	Improved relationships	Increased efficiency
Lower turnover	New opportunity/ venture	Other: _____

IMPLEMENTATION CHECKLIST

The following implementation checklist suggests ways to reduce and address both surprises and conflicts in the future:

1. How can we make this agreement "nearly self-enforcing"? (That is, create incentives for the parties to live up to their commitments.)

2. How will we monitor performance/compliance during the implementation of the agreement?

3. How will we resolve disputes on the interpretation of the information we collect? Who will cover the cost of monitoring and the cost of resolving monitoring disputes?

4. What deadlines or milestones for reconsidering or reconfirming our commitments will we build into the agreement?

5. How will our organizations' incentives and capacities need to change in order to implement this agreement well? How will each of us demonstrate that we're changing?

6. What relationship building commitments can we make to build trust and make it easier to deal with any problems or disagreements that might arise?

7. What dispute resolution mechanisms will we rely on if problems emerge during implementation? Who will activate and/or pay for these?

8. What "predictable surprises" are likely to arise in the course of implementation and what options can we propose to address them?

VIATEX

The simulation called *Viatex* puts participants in groups of two or four (one or two negotiators representing each side). Each person receives general instructions that lay out the scenario and confidential instructions and information relating to their role. The instructions also emphasize the need to meet key financial goals and other organizational interests while protecting relationships with critical partners. Participants are given a chance to review their respective roles and interests, make sense of what has happened in the past, and then negotiate possible new deals.

VIATEX SIMULATION: GENERAL SCENARIO AND INSTRUCTIONS

Brattlebury Corporation, which makes a wide range of pharmaceutical, nutritional, and medical products, purchases supplies from a company called Viatex. Viatex makes plastic bottles in which Brattlebury packages some of its pharmaceutical pills and vitamins for distribution. Viatex has been a supplier to Brattlebury for ten years. During that time, the relationship has been advantageous for both companies. The value of the contract for the last five years has averaged $30 million annually.

In recent years, Brattlebury has faced pressure to cut costs because sales have been flatter than expected. For several years, a strategic sourcing committee (SSC) has worked to find opportunities for business units across Brattlebury to pay less for goods and services. That effort has been successful, although it has not been without conflict: some business units have objected to being told that their current suppliers are suboptimal or overpaid. Last year, in response to a survey of its suppliers, Brattlebury realized that its RFP process was often onerous, and that this inefficiency ended up costing both parties because of the time required to go through a proposal process every two years.

This year, Brattlebury is implementing a method for developing strategic relationships with suppliers that are important to Brattlebury, either because of the size of the contract or because of the importance of the goods they supply. Brattlebury has put Viatex on the list of strategic relationships that it would like to cultivate. Brattlebury is willing to make the following "grand bargain" with its strategic partners: longer contracts (meaning less effort to complete new proposals every two years) in return for reducing Brattlebury's costs by 5 percent annually. In addition, Brattlebury management has agreed to look creatively and collaboratively at ways that it can change Brattlebury specifications and requirements to help strategic suppliers drive down costs.

Last year, Brattlebury represented half of Viatex's business. Viatex has four other clients, and its annual revenues are approximately $60 million, with $5 million in profit. Both sides stand to gain significantly by completing or evaluating RFPs every five years instead of every other year.

Over the last few months, both parties have identified things that could be done to drive down costs. They have assembled a list of improvements, and each has agreed that the steps identified were feasible—in theory. Meanwhile, each side has been trying to assess the actual costs and savings involved with making each one of the changes that have been proposed. The changes are:

- Viatex could do fewer quality control checks at its plant, saving money, if Brattlebury assumed more liability for product defects once bottles were shipped to pharmacists.

- Brattlebury could change bottle specifications so that all bottles ordered from Viatex would come in one of two sizes rather than in one of the five sizes currently produced.

- Brattlebury could take a regular minimum shipment each month. Viatex has been storing bottles at considerable cost in times when Brattlebury has had less need for bottles. Brattlebury has better storage options and rates than Viatex, which is smaller and located in a state with higher storage costs.

- Brattlebury could agree to minimum and maximum quantities for delivery each quarter, which would prevent Viatex from having to lay people off during slow periods and hire and train people during peaks (which is expensive for Viatex).

- Brattlebury could assume responsibility for shipping, as it has very good shipping rates with a private transport company.

- Viatex could use a cheaper plastic made from Resin 242. This new resin is considerably cheaper for Viatex to source than the resin it currently uses, but it carries a slightly higher instance of cracks and blemishes in finished bottles.

In principle, these all seem like good possibilities for saving money and adding value.

Finally, one issue has not yet been discussed: How will joint savings be distributed? Brattlebury has made clear that it must have

5 percent savings per year. This means that for this year, based on a $30 million dollar contract, Brattlebury and Viatex must find $1.5 million for Brattlebury in order to protect the strategic relationship status that Viatex now enjoys.

Today, Brattlebury representative J. Williams and Viatex representative T. Burton are meeting to seek agreement about what steps to take and how savings will be allocated.

Your goal, as one of these parties, is to reach agreement with your counterpart on which initiatives to formalize in the new contract, and how savings will be distributed.

You will have 20 minutes to prepare with those playing the same role and one hour to negotiate an agreement.

CONFIDENTIAL INFORMATION
AND CONSIDERATIONS

In addition to this general background, participants receive confidential instructions describing their interests, constraints, and attitudes in more detail, leaving them with a number of dilemmas to resolve.

In the exercise, there are many possible ways of saving money and adding value. However, it is not obvious how potential joint savings or gains will be distributed between the two sides. Moreover, a lot depends on how each side values each option. Brattlebury wants to achieve 5 percent savings per year. This means that, based on a $30 million dollar contract, Brattlebury and Viatex must find a way to save Brattlebury $1.5 million in order to protect the strategic relationship status Viatex wants to achieve. Yet savings are likely to become available only to the degree that the two sides share confidential information about the benefits and costs that each of the six changes listed above would yield for them.

Brattlebury doesn't know whether (and at what point) Viatex is willing to walk away to other clients in view of the current deal and possible improvements. Viatex doesn't know how much Brattlebury stands to save from administering the RFP process less often, but it wants any savings to be shared. Revealing these details would require a great deal of trust. Also, each side has concerns that the other will get an unfair portion of the greater savings created by sharing such information; this puts strong pressure on both sides not to reveal the confidential information necessary to work out the gains in the first place.

NOTES

Chapter 1

1. As we note in appendix A (which provides a more detailed review of reasons that training fails), organizations in the United States alone spent $134.39 billion in 2007 on employee learning and development, $50.77 billion of which was allocated to external services. If we assume—very conservatively—that training in negotiation might comprise 1 percent of all such training, then in the United States alone, *organizations spent at least $1.3 billion a year on negotiation training.*

2. While we refer throughout this book to companies, we believe our arguments are equally applicable to governmental and nonprofit organizations as well.

Chapter 3

1. Works by these authors include:

Axelrod, Robert. *The Evolution of Cooperation.* New York: Basic Books, 1984.

Bazerman, Max H., and Margaret A. Neale. *Negotiating Rationally.* New York: Free Press, 1992.

Bazerman, Max H., and Michael D. Watkins. *Predictable Surprises: The Disasters You Should Have Seen Coming, and How to Prevent Them.* Boston: Harvard Business School Press, 2004.

Fisher, Roger, and William Ury, with Bruce Patton. *Getting to Yes: Negotiating Agreement Without Giving In*, 2nd ed. New York: Penguin Books, 1991.

Kolb, Deborah M., Judith Williams, and Carol Frohlinger. *Her Place at the Table*: *A Woman's Guide to Negotiating Five Key Challenges to Leadership Success*, 1st ed. San Francisco: Jossey-Bass, 2004.

Lax, David A., and James K. Sebenius. *The Manager as Negotiator*:

Bargaining for Cooperation and Competitive Gain. New York: Free Press, 1986.

———. *3-D Negotiation: Powerful Tools to Change the Game in Your Most Important Deals*. Boston: Harvard Business School Press, 2006.

Mnookin, Robert H., and Lawrence E. Susskind, with Pacey C. Foster, eds. *Negotiating on Behalf of Others: Advice to Lawyers, Business Executives, Sports Agents, Diplomats, Politicians, and Everybody Else*. Thousand Oaks, CA: Sage Publications, 1999.

Mnookin, Robert H., Scott R. Peppet, and Andrew S. Tulumello. *Beyond Winning: Negotiating to Create Value in Deals and Disputes*. Cambridge, MA: Belknap Press of Harvard University Press, 2000.

Raiffa, Howard. *The Art and Science of Negotiation*. Cambridge, MA: Belknap Press of Harvard University Press, 1982.

Schelling, Thomas C. *The Strategy of Conflict*. Cambridge, MA: Harvard University Press, 1960.

Susskind, Lawrence, and Jeffrey Cruikshank. *Breaking the Impasse: Consensual Approaches to Resolving Public Disputes*. New York: Basic Books, 1987.

Susskind, Lawrence, Sarah McKearnan, and Jennifer Thomas-Larmer, eds. *The Consensus Building Handbook: A Comprehensive Guide to Reaching Agreement*. Thousand Oaks, CA: Sage Publications, 1999.

Walton, Richard E., and Robert B. McKersie. *A Behavioral Theory of Labor Negotiation: An Analysis of a Social Interaction System*, 2nd ed. Ithaca, NY: ILR Press, 1991.

Ury, William. *Getting Past No: Negotiating with Difficult People*. New York: Bantam Books, 1991.

2. For a useful treatment of adding, subtracting, and sequencing conversations in negotiation, see Lax and Sebenius, "Thinking Coalitionally: Party Arithmetic, Process Opportunism, and Strategic Sequencing," in H. Peyton Young, ed., *Negotiation Analysis*, (Ann Arbor, MI: University of Michigan Press, 1991).

3. A version of this study was published in the *Negotiation Journal* and can be ordered at http://www3.interscience.wiley.com/journal/118596994/abstract.

4. Kevin Avruch, *Culture and Conflict Resolution* (Washington D.C.: United States Institute of Peace Press, 1998).

5. P. H. Gulliver, *Disputes and Negotiations: A Cross-Cultural Perspective* (New York: Academic Press, 1979).

6. We are careful to say *espoused* because, as we will argue, relying on self-report is always risky.

7. C. Argyris and D. Schon, *Theory in Practice: Increasing Professional Effectiveness* (San Francisco: Jossey Bass, 1974) and *Organisational Learning: A Theory of Action Perspective* (Reading, Mass.: Addison Wesley, 1979).

8. Conversation with authors in 2005.

9. You can take our exam and find out your score for free at http://quiz .cosmicsoft.net/a9r.

10. We provide a longer discussion in appendix A of current thinking about the reasons that training may fail to produce behavior change.

11. Scheduling and conducting interviews, pulling together findings into a draft report for fact checking with interviewees, and then delivering the report can take anywhere from one to three months, depending on the size of the organization, and cost $25,000 to $75,000. The cost of the organizational development effort will vary according to the range of negotiations examined, the numbers of people involved, and the availability of those people to provide time and insight.

Chapter 5

1. D. L. Kirkpatrick, "Techniques for Evaluating Training Programs," *Journal of the ASTD* 13 (1959): 3–9.

2. P. P. Phillips and J. J. Phillips, "11 Reasons Why Training and Development Fails . . . and What You Can Do About It," *Training* 39 (2002): 78–85.

3. American Society for Training and Development, *2004 State of the Industry Report.*

4. Ferdinand Tesoro, "Implementing an ROI Measurement Process at Dell Computer," *Performance Improvement Quarterly* 11 (1998): 103–114.

5. P. T. Coleman and Y.Y. J. Lim, "A Systematic Approach to Evaluating the Effects of Collaborative Negotiation Training on Individuals and Groups," *Negotiation Journal* 17 (2001): 363–392.

6. For a review, see H. Movius, "The Effectiveness of Negotiation Training," *Negotiation Journal* (October 2008): 509–531.

7. J. Collins, *Good to Great: Why Some Companies Make the Leap . . . and Others Don't* (New York: Collins Publishing, 2001).

8. The idea that value creation is affected by the cognitive abilities of individual negotiators derives from B. Barry and R. A. Friedman, "Bargainer Characteristics in Distributive and Integrative Negotiation," *Journal of Personality and Social Psychology* 74 (1998): 345–359.

9. J. Nadler, L. Thompson, and L. Van Boven, "Learning Negotiation

Skills: Four Models of Knowledge Creation and Transfer," *Management Science* 49 (2003): 529–540.

10. M. A. Steinman, M. G. Shlipak, S. J. McPhee, "Of Principles and Pens: Attitudes and Practices of Medicine Housestaff Toward Pharmaceutical Industry Promotions," *American Journal of Medicine* (May 2001): 551–557.

11. W. G. Bennis, *On Becoming a Leader* (New York: Basis Books, 2003).

12. D. A. Lax and J. K. Sebenius, *3-D Negotiation* (Cambridge: Harvard Business School Press, 2006), 16.

13. "Win" is widely used and referred to as a generic exercise, but a version is owned by the PON Clearinghouse.

14. L. Ross and A. Ward, "Naïve Realism: Implications for Social Conflict and Misunderstanding," in T. Brown, E. Reed, and E. Turiel, eds., *Values and Knowledge* (Hillsdale, N.J.: Laurence Erlbaum Associates, 1996).

15. M. Rokeach, *The Open and Closed Mind: Investigations into the Nature of Belief Systems and Personality Systems* (New York: Basic Books, 1973).

16. Reggie Van Lee, Lisa Fabish, Nancy McGaw, "The Value of Corporate Values," *Strategy and Business* (Summer 2005: 55–58, 60–61). See http://www.strategy-business.com/article/05206?gko=7869b-1876-9176155.

17. These findings are from Joseph H. Bragdon, *Profit for Life: How Capitalism Excels* (Cambridge, Mass.: Society for Organizational Learning, 2006).

18. J. R. Curhan, H. A. Elfenbein, and H. Xu, "What Do People Value When They Negotiate? Mapping the Domain of Subjective Valuation in Negotiation," *Journal of Personality and Social Psychology* 91(3) (2006): 493–512.

19. Sandra E. Cha and Amy C. Edmondson, "When Values Backfire: Leadership, Attribution, and Disenchantment in a Values-Driven Organization," *The Leadership Quarterly* 17 (2006): 57–78.

20. Van Lee, Fabish, McGaw, "The Value of Corporate Values."

21. John R. Graham, R. Harvey Campbell, and Rajgopal Shivaram, "The Economic Implications of Corporate Financial Reporting," *Journal of Accounting and Economics* 40 (2005): 3–73.

22. These recommendations from Dean Krehmeyer, Matthew Orsagh, and Kurt N. Schacht, *Breaking the Short-Term Cycle: Discussion and Recommendations on How Corporate Leaders, Asset Managers, Investors, and Analysts Can Refocus on Long-Term Value* (CFA Institute, Business Roundtable Institute for Corporate Ethics, 2006). Full report available at http://www.corporate-ethics.org/.

23. Peggy Hsieh, Timothy Koller, and S. R. Rajan, "The Misguided Practice of Earnings Guidance," *McKinsey Quarterly* (March 2006).

Appendix A

1. H. Raiffa, *The Art and Science of Negotiation* (Cambridge, Mass.: Belknap Press, 1982); R. Fisher and W. Ury, *Getting to Yes: Negotiating Agreement Without Giving In* (Boston: Houghton Mifflin, 1981).

2. American Society for Training and Development (ASTD) in its *2008 State of the Industry Report.*

3. H. Movius, "The Effectiveness of Negotiation Training," *Negotiation Journal* (October 2008): 509–531.

4. For reviews, see Max H. Bazerman and Margaret A. Neale, *Negotiating Rationally* (New York: Free Press, 1992); L. Thompson, *The Mind and Heart of the Negotiator* (Upper Saddle River, N.J.: Pearson Prentice Hall, 2005); M. B. Bazerman, J. R. Curhan, D. A. Moore, and K. L. Valley, "Negotiation," *Annnual Review of Psychology* 51 (2000): 279–314; R. J. Lewicki, D. M. Saunders, and J. W. Minton, *Negotiation,* 5th ed (Boston: McGraw-Hill Higher Education, 2005).

5. For reviews, see L. Thompson, "Negotiation Behavior and Outcomes: Empirical Evidence and Theoretical Issues," *Psychological Bulletin* 108 (1990): 515–532; Bazerman and Neale, *Negotiating Rationally*; Lewicki et al., *Negotiation.*

6. Interestingly, attributing others' behavior to traits or beliefs appears to occur more often and powerfully in situations involving individuals from Western cultures, which have a collectivistic rather than individualist orientation.

7. While there are examples in the laboratory of "debiasing" by teaching subjects about specific cognitive pitfalls (e.g., Bazerman and Neale, *Negotiating Rationally*), the laboratory situations were sufficiently controlled and artificial that we doubt whether subjects would be able to consistently avoid bias in more complicated and competitive situations. And other studies have found that even cash awards for being fair do not prevent people from making self-serving judgments about what outcome is "fair."

L. Babcock and G. Loewenstein, "Explaining Bargaining Impasse: The Role of Self-Serving Biases," *Journal of Economic Perspectives* 11 (1997): 109–126. Linda Babcock, George Loewenstein, Samuel Issacharoff and Colin Camerer, "Biased Judgments of Fairness in Bargaining," *The American Economic Review* 85 (December 1995): 1337–1343. E. Pronin, T. D. Gilovich, and L. Ross, "Objectivity in the Eye of the Beholder: Divergent

Perceptions of Bias in Self Versus Others," *Psychological Review* 111 (2004); 781–799. E. Pronin, D. Y. Lin, and L. Ross, "The Bias Blind Spot: Perceptions of Bias in Self Versus Others" *Personality and Social Psychology Bulletin* 28 (2002): 369–381.

8. For reviews, see Jeffrey Z. Rubin and Bert R. Brown, *The Social Psychology of Bargaining and Negotiation* (New York: Academic Press, 1975) and D. G. Pruitt and J. Z. Rubin, *Social Conflict: Escalation, Stalemate and Settlement* (New York: McGraw-Hill, 1986); Raiffa, *The Art and Science of Negotiation*; Thompson, *The Mind and Heart of the Negotiator*.

9. L. Ross and A. Ward, "Naïve Realism: Implications for Social Conflict and Misunderstanding," in T. Brown, E. Reed, and E. Turiel, eds., *Values and Knowledge* (Hillsdale, N.J.: Laurence Erlbaum Associates, 1996); L. Ross and R. E. Nisbett, *The Person and the Situation: Perspectives of Social Psychology* (Philadelphia: Temple University Press, 1991).

10. Daniel Gilbert, *Stumbling on Happiness* (New York: Knopf, 2006); Timothy Wilson, *Strangers to Ourselves: Discovering the Adaptive Unconscious* (Cambridge, Mass.: Belknap, 2004).

11. J. Nadler, L. Thompson, and L. van Boven, "Learning Negotiation Skills: Four Models of Knowledge Creation and Transfer," *Management Science* 49 (2003): 529–540.

12. Albert Bandura, *Social Learning Theory* (Englewood Cliffs, N.J.: Prentice Hall, 1977).

A GLOSSARY OF THE
MUTUAL GAINS APPROACH

Best alternative to a negotiated agreement (BATNA): Your next best option (sometimes estimated based on weighted probabilities) if no agreement is reached.

Contingent commitments: Commitments taking the form of "if . . ., then . . ." statements; used to cope with different beliefs about the future or to reward or penalize performance or compliance.

Dispute resolution mechanisms: Voluntary arrangements incorporated into agreements spelling out how noncompliance or perceptions of nonperformance will be confronted and resolved.

Fractionating: The breaking of a single issue into multiple issues.

Interests: The kinds of things the negotiating parties care about, in rank order. Interests can be substantive, procedural, or psychological.

Nearly self-enforcing agreement: Deals that both sides are eager to implement because their interests have been met and they have incorporated incentives and controls that make noncompliance foolish.

Objective criteria: Suggested standards or reasons that any neutral observer might use to judge the fairness or reasonableness of specific proposals or packages.

Options for mutual gain: Trades across two or more issues that exploit differences in what parties value or can deliver.

Packages: Bundles of options (across all issues) designed to address the parties' interests

Playing the game of "What if?": The process of inventing or brainstorming packages or possible trades without any implied commitments.

Positions: Stated demands.

Reservation price: The point at which you are indifferent to walking away (i.e., the least you will accept or most you will provide, based on your alternatives away from the table).

Second (or back) table(s): The people (not at the table) to whom you report or who must give their approval to any deal you make.

Zone of possible agreement (ZOPA): The negotiating space (if there is any) created by your reservation price and the reservation price of the other side.

INDEX

ABOUT THE AUTHORS

HALLAM MOVIUS is principal at the Consensus Building Institute; co-instructor for the Program on Technology Negotiation (an executive seminar offered through the Program on Negotiation at Harvard Law School); and visiting associate professor at the University of Virginia's Darden School of Business. Trained as a social and clinical psychologist, he helps leaders and organizations improve negotiation processes and results and deal with the psychological biases and interpersonal patterns that can derail negotiations. Dr. Movius has published papers on leadership, negotiation, the effectiveness of negotiation training, negotiating cross-cultural business deals, and dealing with difficult counterparts, as well as dozens of negotiation simulations and cases. He has delivered workshops and worked with companies in the United States, Mexico, Canada, Singapore, Spain, France, Switzerland, Germany, Holland, England, Peru, and Brazil. He lives in Virginia with his wife and children, and tries hard to keep his guitars from gathering dust.

LAWRENCE SUSSKIND is a professor at the Massachusetts Institute of Technology (MIT), where he has been a member of the faculty for more than thirty-five years. In the early 1980s, he helped to found the Program on Negotiation (PON) at Harvard Law School. Susskind continues to serve as vice-chair for instruction at PON and oversees its executive training programs. More than thirty thousand business executives and public sector managers have participated in trainings that Professor Susskind has designed and delivered. In 1993, he founded the Consensus Building Institute (CBI), a not-for-profit organization that mediates some of the most complicated public disputes around the world and provides tailored negotiation and dispute resolution training. Susskind is the author of twenty books, including the award-winning *Dealing with an Angry Public* (1996) and the *Consensus Building Handbook* (1999). His recent book, *Breaking Robert's Rules: A New Way to Run Your Meeting, Build Consensus and Get Results* (2006), has been published in seven languages.